Nature is all around us, in the beautiful but also in the unappealing and functional, and from the awe-inspiring to the mundane. It is vital that we learn to see the agency of the natural world in all things that make our lives possible, comfortable and profitable. *The Ecology of Everyday Things* pulls back the veil of our familiarity on a range of 'everyday things' that surround us, and which we perhaps take too much for granted. This key into the magic world of the everyday can enable us to take better account of our common natural inheritance.

Professor James Longhurst, Assistant Vice Chancellor,
University of the West of England (UWE Bristol)

When people talk about 'celebrating nature', they usually have dramatic landscapes or charismatic creatures in mind. Mark Everard invites us to celebrate nature in the everyday, in the common places of our lives, and provides lots of information and inspiration along the way.

Jonathon Porritt, Founder Director of Forum for the Future

Mark Everard invites us to look a little closer at, and think a little harder about, the natural architecture of our cultural selves … instructive and entertaining.

Dr Robert Fish, Reader in Human Ecology, University of Kent

If you want to discover more about how intrinsically linked we are to our planet, then *The Ecology of Everyday Things* will open your eyes into how nature underpins everything in our daily lives. In this insightful new book, Mark Everard brings alive his personal observations of the things most of us fail to notice in our everyday activities and simple daily pleasures. From turning on a tap of water to pouring a pint of beer, Everard challenges us to contemplate the 'real value' of nature. Our society is increasingly aware of the importance of nature to better support our health and wellbeing, and it is our sense of a relationship with the natural world that is a vital element of this. Everard exposes this in an approachable way through his descriptions of the everyday activities that engage our senses, emotions, compassion and appreciation of beauty – bringing out a personal meaning for each of us – and developing our connections with nature.

Amanda Craig, Director, People & Nature, Natural England

D0992605

THE ECOLOGY OF
EVERYDAY THINGS

THE ECOLOGY OF EVERYDAY THINGS

Mark Everard

CRC Press
Taylor & Francis Group
Boca Raton London New York

CRC Press is an imprint of the
Taylor & Francis Group, an **informa** business

First edition published 2021
by CRC Press
6000 Broken Sound Parkway NW, Suite 300, Boca Raton, FL 33487-2742

and by CRC Press
2 Park Square, Milton Park, Abingdon, Oxon, OX14 4RN

© 2021 Taylor & Francis Group, LLC

CRC Press is an imprint of Taylor & Francis Group, LLC

ISBN: 978-0-367-63634-0 (hbk)
ISBN: 978-0-367-63631-9 (pbk)
ISBN: 978-1-003-12005-6 (ebk)

Typeset in Times New Roman
by MPS Limited, Dehradun

Contents

Acknowledgements

Many thanks to those from whom I have learned: from philosophers and writers to scientific and media colleagues, my family and friends here and overseas, and the many people from all walks of life who – whether they know it or not – have given me cause to pause and look anew at the magic latent in everyday things.

Thanks also to you, who may find inspiration and go forward to change the world for the better.

About the Author

Mark Everard, PhD, is Associate Professor of Ecosystem Services at the University of the West of England (UWE Bristol), as well as a consultant, broadcaster and author. He is also Vice-President of the Institution of Environmental Sciences, a Fellow of the Linnaean Society, an Angling Trust Ambassador, and a science advisor to Salmon & Trout Conservation UK, Tiger Watch (India), Wiltshire Wildlife Trust and a range of other bodies.

Completing his PhD in water and wetlands, Dr Everard has since substantially broadened his work across Europe, the developing world (particularly India/South Asia and both East and South Africa) and other global regions to recognise the integral connections between ecosystems and the social and economic wellbeing of people. His work has been in government, academic, broadcast and media, private consultancy and NGO settings, and across five continents.

Dr Everard's mission now is to help society re-integrate this understanding of the intimate connection between our activities and policies with the much-degraded natural world. It is to provoke and inspire change in our perspectives, policies, industrial processes and habits, developing new ways of living that rebuild nature's vital life support systems. These systems have not only supported our evolution, but are the most fundamental of resources underpinning future human security, prosperity and opportunity. He is also a passionate fisherman and naturalist, frequently appearing in magazines, as well as on television and radio.

Selected Relevant Books by Mark Everard

- Everard, M. (2020). *Rebuilding the Earth: Regenerating Our Planet's Life Support Systems for a Sustainable Future*. Palgrave Macmillan: London and New York.
- Everard, M. with photographs by Jack Perks (2020). *The Complex Lives of British Freshwater Fishes*. CRC/Taylor & Francis: Boca Raton, FL.
- Everard, M. (2018). *Riverwatch: The Waterside Diaries of a Naturalist-Angler*. Hobnob Press: Gloucester.
- Everard, M. (2017). *Ecosystem Services: Key Issues*. Routledge: London and New York.
- Everard, M. (2016). *The Ecosystems Revolution: Co-creating a Symbiotic Future*, Palgrave Pivot Series. Palgrave Macmillan: London and New York.
- Everard, M. (2015). *Breathing Space: The Natural and Unnatural History of Air*. Zed Books: London.
- Everard, M. (2015). *River Habitats for Coarse Fish: How Fish Use Rivers and How We Can Help Them*. Old Pond Publishing: Sheffield.
- Everard, M. (2013). *The Hydropolitics of Dams: Engineering or Ecosystems?* Zed Books: London.
- Everard, M. (2013). *Britain's Freshwater Fishes*. Princeton University Press/WildGUIDES: Princeton, NJ.
- Everard, M. and Knight, P. (2013). *Britain's Game Fishes: Celebration and Conservation of Salmonids*. Pelagic Press: Totnes.
- Everard, M. (2012). *Fantastic Fishes: A Feast of Facts and Fables*. Medlar Press: Ellesmere.
- Everard, M. (2011). *Common Ground: The Sharing of Land and Landscapes for Sustainability*. Zed Books: London.
- Everard, M. (2009). *The Business of Biodiversity*. WIT Publishing: Hampshire.
- Everard, M. (2008). *The Little Book of Little Fishes*. Medlar Press: Ellesmere.

1 The Nature of Modern Society

We live in an era of unprecedented technological miracles. If we could pluck someone from mediaeval times and drop them into our homes today, I am sure we would blow their minds (and not merely about the achievement of time travel).

This temporally displaced person would wonder that water is piped into our homes, available hot or cold at any time of day or night and in any season, and that our wastewater is magically spirited away when we are done with it. They would be stunned that there was little or no seasonality to the food we buy and consume, with exotic and staple foodstuffs — including non-indigenous products that have today become staples — available not only year-round but also 24/7 and even delivered to our doors on demand. Also, of course, that we could demand things of that nature through the apparent power of telepathy granted us by telephones and computers. That power comes conveniently and dependably through plug sockets in every room for our utility, to light rooms at nightfall, play music at the push of a button and run televisions, computers, dishwaters and vacuum cleaners, would appear to be sorcery.

Imagine how this person would react when feeling unwell, not having to run to the river to find leeches to let blood to oust the disease but instead offered a choice of remedies from a veritable pharmacopeia of pills and potions kept handy to tackle a variety of ailments. And how would our fictional time traveller react to the astounding comfort of our homes, well-insulated against draughts and storms, rain and snow, frost and heat-waves, warmed or cooled at the twist of a dial? They would wonder at the fact that few of us go hungry, selecting from a smorgasbord of specialty foods from five continents where they were formerly reserved only as festival dishes. They might be surprised that we don't smell, or at least that we can choose to wash (or not) as and when we like, night or day, not by trekking down to an icy river but from water plumbed right into our homes and warmed for our comfort.

Perhaps we too should marvel more often at how our near-miraculous yet now commonplace built infrastructure has given us access to nature's richness within our own homes. All these technologically enabled domestic conveniences exist for the simple purposes of plugging us into a deeper and more fundamental 'natural infrastructure': the cycles and flows of nature's resources, upon which we depend utterly yet may give little or no thought. The ease with which we now access these ultimately natural products and flows tends to dull awareness of our continuing dependency upon nature in meeting our daily needs.

Like all of nature, we interact with all of nature in the ways we eat, breathe, drink and excrete, and in the other myriad ways in which we meet our needs and demands. We have great ingenuity in manipulating the natural world to meet our demands, from agricultural and industrial production to river engineering, forestry, construction, energy harvesting and in so many other ways. To some extent, we are not alone in this, as many other creatures manipulate natural systems to promote their own ends. For example, beavers in Europe and North America dam rivers and divert flows for protection and to increase feeding opportunities, African elephants push down trees to maintain open grazing sward in savannah and forest fringes, ants 'herd' and protect aphids to benefit from their secretions of 'honeydew' tapped from the sugars in the veins of plants, and parasites of all types exploit other organisms as sources of nutrition, protection, transport and transmission. Indeed, it is the collective action of all living things that maintains the atmosphere, which recycles gases and distributes spores and chemical signals, and which shields us from damaging radiation from space, thereby making the continuation of life possible on this small blue sphere cart-wheeling through the dark void of space. Like all of nature, we are indivisibly connected — down to the finest organelles and biochemicals in each of the cells of our bodies — with all of nature with which we co-evolved.

We too manipulate natural systems to promote our own advantage. However, the sheer range and scale of humanity's capacity to manipulate ecosystems for our own ends has no parallels elsewhere in nature. We have re-plumbed water flows across entire subcontinents to serve burgeoning cities and thirsty farming and industrial activities. We have appropriated the productive capacities of some 24% of the land surface of this planet for our own exclusive use, sweeping away the complex habitats and ecosystems that have evolved there over millions of years along with the diversity of benefits they confer in terms of stabilising the climate, recycling and regenerating energy and matter, buffering and purifying water, supporting wildlife of inherent and also recreational and aesthetic value, amongst a host of other natural processes. We have tamed and selectively bred some animals for food, muscle power, decoration, protection or companionship. At the same time, mushrooming human numbers and our associated demands for resources have driven other creatures that may be potential predators, pests or competitors to scarcity or extinction. We have also been merciless with organisms that could be a source or vector of human, stock or crop diseases, using control methods often with a far wider 'footprint' of ecological damage. We have, in short, profoundly changed the face of the Earth, its waters, the stability of its climate system, and the balance and nature of its ecosystems.

However, this book is not about environmental crisis or its solutions: see various of my other books for those studies of environmentalist existentialism! Instead, it is about celebration. You see, those everyday technological miracles, so familiar to us yet which would spin the head of someone from another era of history, in no way dissociate us from our fundamentally biological roots. All of those familiar technologies are, in one way or another, merely ingenious ways to channel the benefits of cooling river flows, natural energy, and nature's nutritious and remedial qualities to support and ease our emancipated modern lifestyles. But nature is still always there, supplying the goods and taking out the trash as far as its capacities allow, however remotely connected to it we are by sophisticated chains of technology which themselves are made from and powered by nature's materials and flows.

Apart from our biological nature, it is also in the nature of humanity to innovate and learn. This is nowhere more manifest than in the technological wonders of modern life, from the everyday bar of soap to the loaf of bread that we take so much for granted, as indeed in the life support systems of the International Space Station. Sadly, and with major consequences, it has also become part of the nature of modern society to forget our inherent and indivisible rootedness in the natural world, and that our technical prowess in accessing it has to be considered and reformed with far more informed far-sightedness about its wider impacts.

Sometimes, we take ourselves off to extraordinary places to experience the rawness, the awesomeness of nature. Whether as a physical experience, or vicariously via television, other media or in a flight of the mind, we might experience the surging flows of a powerful river, feel the vigour of a fresh-run salmon on our fishing line, stride on a mountain ridge fighting for a footing against a buffeting wind, scuba dive amongst corals draped in near-psychedelic marine creatures, or watch dumb-struck at the spectacle of migrating waders spiralling over a desolate salt marsh. Nature in the wild is, undoubtedly, exhilarating and life-affirming, touching us deeply and so connecting us with parts of ourselves that are both of kind with it but also for too long buried by a raft of daily pressures. It is inspiring to connect with life, and thus to feel once again alive.

But this book is a celebration of the ecology not of the remote and the exotic, but of everyday things. It opens a window to look at everything from a simple cup of tea, a bath of water, a bowl of rice, a newspaper, a wasp and a pile of dirt with a little less familiarity, and to see how nature is as present in the mundane and the everyday — even in space travel — as it is so evidently in a safari to the plains of Africa.

It is perhaps a symptom of disconnection from the natural world consequent from daily exigencies that we miss these close yet over-familiar connections with nature in the day-to-day. From the paper upon which this book is printed to the ink imprint of its letters, the energy and water entailed in the production of both or the powering of the eReader device, in the wool in my pullover and in the regeneration by remote but incessantly busy plankton and forests of the air we breathe, nature is always underwriting our wellbeing in so far as its currently damaged capacities allow.

As the title of this book suggests, *The Ecology of Everyday Things* is all about seeing nature in the world around us. And, who knows, by seeing the world differently and touching our rootedness in nature, we may enrich and inform our own lives, our ensuing decisions, and thereby also contribute to the safeguarding of prospects for the myriad people with whom we are unbreakably interconnected by our common ecological dependences.

2 Reading the Tea Leaves

Thinking about all this stuff can make you thirsty. For me, that usually calls for making a cup of tea, and kicking back a moment to reflect.

Pausing a moment, one can see, hear, smell and otherwise sense nature all around us. We hear it in the song of birds and the rustle of wind amongst leaves and twigs. Even from the tallest of tower blocks, we see cloudscapes, the flight of birds, raindrops on the windows and the canopies of trees far below. But the air we are breathing is also nature, as are the various processes that cleanse and regenerate it. We eat nature, no matter how processed the end results that end up on our plates. It is nature that then purifies and recycles the wastes from our bodies, even where we apply sewage treatment technologies to decontaminate the most concentrated pollutants using engineering to increase the pace of the physical, chemical and biological processes of the natural world. It is nature also that closes the loop by regenerating our spent resources into new food and other biological productivity. And it is nature's processes that moderate the climate, recycle nutrients and water, and that regenerate the soils that produce 90% of our food. And, of course, nature pervades the cup of tea around which I am warming my hands.

THE NATURE OF TEA

There are many forms of tea. My favourite tipple is Rooibos tea, made from the dried leaves of a dryland fynbos plant known as red bush (*Aspalathus linearis*) from

South Africa. But, for the current purpose, let's just think about everyday black 'builder's tea'.

Now this tea is very much a product of the Earth. The tea that we put in our teapots or in teabags is derived from the tea plant (*Camellia sinensis*), which occurs naturally in China where it has been cultivated for human use for centuries. The black tea familiar in the West is a cured and crumbled form of the tea plant's leaves, its darkness resulting from the breakdown of chlorophyll to produce tannins.

In its uncured form, green tea has long been ascribed a variety of properties beneficial to human health. Indeed, the health effects of infusions from the tea plant have been exploited and explored since around 4,700 years ago, when China's legendary emperor Shennong claimed, in *The Divine Farmer's Herb-Root Classic*, that they were useful in the treatment of a range of medical conditions that included abscesses, bladder ailments, lethargy and tumours.[1]

The biological activity of the tea plant, or indeed any plant, should not be a surprise. You see, one of the interesting challenges faced by plants, rooted plants in particular, arises from the fact that they cannot run away from things that want to eat or infect them, nor uproot themselves to cosy up to others of their kind. As part of their remarkable survival strategies, modern plants have been imbued by evolution with an impressive array of chemical defence, communication and hormonal systems. Remarkably, plants also synthesise this fantastic complexity and diversity of chemicals at background temperatures, in water, and generating no residual waste, forging them from no more than water, air, sunlight and nutrients from the soil. We have serious lessons to learn from the everyday alchemy of plants when we contrast that with our own high-temperature, high-energy chemical manufacturing processes often in exotic solvents with all sorts of potentially polluting by-products.

Some of these plant-generated, biologically active chemicals manifest as poisons, odours that may be pleasant or repulsive, or as substances with herbal or medicinal benefits. Humanity has made wide use of many of these beneficial properties. Various traditional medicine practices based on the properties of herbs rely directly on the 'genetic intelligence' encoded by plants as a product of 3.85 billion years of evolution. So too does a large proportion of modern drugs, including also the substantial number of manufactured drugs that replicate or are modified forms of the structures and properties of naturally produced molecules. And, of course, we co-evolved as part of this network of ecological interactions.

Scientific research has confirmed some of the beneficial properties of green tea for humans, many of them related to its powerful antioxidant properties. (For the detail lovers amongst us, like me, one of the most significant antioxidant constituents are the catechins, which can comprise up to 30% of the dry weight of freshly picked tea leaves.[2]) The range of observed health benefits includes reducing

---

[1] Woodward, N.H. (1980). *Teas of the World*. Collier Books: University of California.

[2] Lee, K.W., Lee, H.J. and Lee, C.Y. (2002). Antioxidant activity of black tea vs. green tea. *Journal of Nutrition*, 132(4), p. 785.

blood pressure and risks of cardiovascular disease as well as some types of cancer, assisting with management of weight, antibacterial and antiviral properties and some protection from ultraviolet radiation,[3] in addition to neuroprotective qualities.[4] Substances in tea known as catechins also react with the same cellular mechanisms that are receptive to cannabinoids (a group of chemicals including the active ingredients of the cannabis plant) and which affect cellular mechanisms in ways that suppress pain and nausea, explaining at least some of the overall calming effects of tea.[5]

These qualities, in addition to the slightly bitter taste and astringent properties released when infused in boiling water, meant that tea was initially regarded as a medicinal drink in China. However, the wider global enjoyment of tea as a beverage came first to Europe with Portuguese priests and merchants returning from China during the 16th century, with tea consumption becoming increasingly popular in Britain during the 17th century. It is the British who had a major role in spreading the plant itself beyond China, appropriating the tea plant and introducing it to India in order to break China's trading monopoly.

THE CULTURE AND POLITICS OF TEA

Today, the humble tea plant has been transplanted to soils across the world, mainly in the tropics and subtropics but even locally and with limited success in some temperate ones including southern England and Wales. In 2010, world tea production reached over 4.52 million tonnes,[6] with the largest tea-producing nations including China, India, Kenya, Sri Lanka and Turkey. The tea trade is therefore massive, supporting an industry worth £629 million in the UK alone.[7] Many strains of tea bushes are grown across this range, and the leaves are processed in a variety of different ways including, in particular, various levels of curing controlled by heat. Today, tea is the second most consumed beverage on Earth after water, and it is also globally the most popular manufactured drink in terms of the quantities consumed, outstripping all other manufactured drinks in the world combined.[8]

Aside from its cultural importance in trade, various ceremonies are associated with tea-drinking across a range of cultures. These range from the famous ritualised tea ceremonies of Japan and China, through to its role in 'polite society' tea parties

---

[3] Heinrich, U., Moore, C.E., Tronnier, H. and Stahl, W. (2011). Green tea polyphenols provide photoprotection, increase microcirculation, and modulate skin properties of women. *Journal of Nutrition,* 141(6), pp. 1202–1208.

[4] Cabrera, C., Artacho, R. and Giménez, R. (2006). Beneficial effects of green tea: a review. *Journal of the American College of Nutrition,* 25(2), pp. 79–99.

[5] Korte, G. *et al.* (2010). Tea catechins' affinity for human cannabinoid receptors. *Phytomedicine,* 17(1), pp. 19–22.

[6] Agritrade Executive Brief on Tea, 2013. (https://agritrade.cta.int/Agriculture/Commodities/Tea/Executive-Brief-Update-2013-Tea-sector.html, accessed 26 May 2020.)

[7] Weston, S. (2013). Global tea industry 'is in crisis' says Caf'direct. Foodbev.com, 19 June 2013. (https://www.foodbev.com, accessed 26 May 2020.)

[8] Macfarlane, A. and Macfarlane I. (2004). *The Empire of Tea.* Overlook Press. p. 32. ISBN 1–58567-493-1.

and working class tea breaks in the Western world. By contrast, in the United States and Canada, 80% of tea is consumed as iced tea.

Furthermore, tea has enjoyed moments of political significance throughout history. These range from widespread tea smuggling during the 18th century, giving Britain's masses access to a beverage formerly reserved for the wealthy, to the Boston Tea Party which subsequently escalated into the American Revolution when demonstrators masquerading as native American 'Indians' destroyed an entire shipment of tea in defiance of the Tea Act of 1773, which controlled its trade. More recent political protests in the United States since 2010 are also known as the Tea Party movement, referring back to the Boston Tea Party in their promotion of an agenda of cutting both taxes and public spending.

Tea thus has an amazing nexus of geographical, economic, ceremonial and political connotations. However, my tea today is made with boiling water and with no ritual beyond the dunking of a teabag into the mug.

IN HOT WATER

The third-of-a-pint or so of hot water in which the tea is infused has also been on an extraordinary journey to reach its temporary residence in my cup. Perhaps this is a journey and a substance that we should treat with a little more respect each time we turn on the tap to fill the kettle, as a substantial proportion of the water on the planet today is made up from the materials from which the Earth was formed,[9,10] coalescing into liquid form as the early Earth cooled as long as 4.4 billion years ago, shortly after the formation of the planet. Some more of this water might have originated from comets and from protoplanets formed in the outer asteroid belt, and which subsequently plunged to Earth early in its history.[11] So that colourless, odourless fluid that we take for granted has been with us since (at least) the birth of the planet, continuously recirculated and cleansed by physical and biological processes and residing, just for this minute or two, in my mug to dissolve the tea.

That third-of-a-pint of fresh water is also a remarkably scarce thing. Though seemingly abundant on a planet with a surface 71% covered by water, and with a blue aura produced in large measure by moisture in the atmosphere, fresh water comprises only 2.5% of the Earth's 332,500,000 cubic miles (1,386,000,000 cubic kilometres) of water resources. Furthermore, most of this fresh water is locked away as snow and ice, with substantial volumes inaccessible in deep aquifers (underground reserves). This leaves only some 0.007% of all the water on Earth accessible for direct human uses in lakes, rivers, reservoirs and those underground sources shallow enough to be accessed affordably. The global water resource is also far from static, recycling constantly through the atmosphere, land surfaces and

[9] Drake, M.J. (2005). Origin of water in the terrestrial planets. *Meteoritics & Planetary Science*, 40(4), pp. 519–527.

[10] Drake, M.J. *et al.* (2005). Origin of water in the terrestrial planets. *Asteroids, Comets, and Meteors (IAU S229)*. 229th Symposium of the International Astronomical Union, 1(4). Búzios, Rio de Janeiro, Brazil: Cambridge University Press. pp. 381–394.

[11] Morbidelli, A. *et al.* (2000). Source regions and timescales for the delivery of water to the Earth. *Meteoritics & Planetary Science*, 35, pp. 1309–1329.

vegetation and fauna, underground aquifers, surface pools, wetlands and streams, estuaries and the open sea.

So, savour every drop! (We will explore a little more of the magic and mystery of water later, in Chapter 6, *Bath Time*.)

Of course, energy inputs are required to boil the water in order to infuse the tea. I guess I could have burned a few twigs from my garden to boil the water in my Kelly Kettle, releasing solar energy captured by photosynthetic processes and locked up in the chemical structure of wood. But I didn't do this today, opting instead for the lazier path of filling the kettle from the tap (not the river) then plugging it into the mains. But the flow of power from the electricity socket is no less a product of nature.

Our chosen electricity supplier has an exclusively 'green' tariff, undertaking to build at least as much renewable energy-generating capacity as its customers consume. This makes a positive contribution to Britain's increasing installed renewable energy generation capacity. However, the reality remains that what actually flows through to the kettle from the socket is a mix of energy sources in proportion to what is fed regionally into the National Grid. Where we live, that mix includes a substantial proportion of power from coal-fired power stations with some additional nuclear and wind generated sources.

In some regards, the coal-powered electricity is similar to the other option of burning twigs harvested from the garden. After all, coal is merely fossilised plant matter formed from the remains of dense swamp forests, much of which grew 300–400 million years ago. These plants were rooted in a very different world from that with which we are familiar. *Meganeura*, giant insects related to modern-day dragonflies but with wingspans up to 65 centimetres (over two feet), hawked the air whilst some fish species had adapted to walk on land giving rise to the earliest amphibians and reptiles, ultimately leading on to the rise of dinosaurs, birds and mammals. Sometimes, coal is referred to as 'buried sunshine' as the bonds of the chemical substances from which it is composed result from the capture of solar radiation in these ancient and alien forests, dying vegetation sinking into and becoming buried in swampy areas (see later, Chapter *Fossilised Sunbeams*.) The immense weight and pressure resulting over many years from burial of peat by newer rock strata as the Earth aged progressively served to squeeze out water, compressing it to as much as one-tenth of its thickness, and rising temperatures also triggered a range of chemical transformations. It is this density of organic matter that means that coal is also 'energy dense', producing a substantial energy output per unit weight when burned (compared to the fresh twig from my garden). And it is for this reason that coal is used by people for so many things, from the fire in the living room hearth to it being the largest global source of energy exploited today for electricity generation.[12]

The burning of coal unleashes all those 'fossilised sunbeams' for which we have so many uses. However, energy is just one element of what is stored and then

---

[12] Energy Information Administration. (2008). *International Energy Annual 2006*. Energy Information Administration (Archived from the original on 23 May 2011).

subsequently released when coal is burned today. Coal-burning also unlocks vast reserves of carbon captured from carbon dioxide gas in the early Earth atmosphere, fused with water by those ancient plants to build complex chemicals by using solar energy to fuse atmospheric carbon dioxide with water. It is this return to the atmosphere of large amounts of carbon formerly locked away in the Earth's crust that is today contributing to the phenomenon of global warming, in effect returning the atmosphere towards an earlier phase of planetary climate and evolution, and hence giving rise to major concerns for the future.

Other problems arising from the contemporary scale of coal-burning relate to the release of a range of fine particulates and other potentially problematic substances into the atmosphere. In the United States alone, waste gases from coal-fired power plants are believed to cause nearly 24,000 premature deaths annually,[13] with annual health costs in Europe stemming from the use of coal to generate electricity assessed in 2013 as running at €42.8 billion ($US 46.7 billion at current rate of conversion).[14]

However, our purpose in this chapter is not to lecture on the environmental issues associated with current energy generation and the consequent need for cleaner sources of energy, including reducing the amount of energy that we consume. Rather, it is to discover just how remarkable a fact it is that the warmth I feel from the cup of tea between my palms was captured from sunlight by ancient forests of giant horse-tails, club mosses, scale trees and ferns, stalked by giant amphibians as long as 6 metres (18 feet) as well as the 9 centimetre-long (3½-inch) forebears of modern cockroaches.

The principal differences between obtaining energy by burning twigs from the garden and using electricity generated through coal-burning are ones of scale: both of vast differences in time span and in terms of the sheer volume of biomass involved. So yes, the fossil energy now converted to heat in my mug of tea is as much a product of nature as the greenery I can see right now out of the window, differing only in that it was captured from the rays of a sun shining on and becoming locked away into chemical bonds in organic matter by ancestral vegetation in the Carboniferous era of Earth's long history. Today's vegetation will, in like manner, store some of the carbon liberated once again through the burning of coal, locking it away into fresh biomass using energy captured from the sun's rays. However, a lot more of the carbon dioxide released will continue to accumulate in the atmosphere, contributing to an increasing greenhouse effect.

As a visible and positive contributor to the generation of energy with less associated environmental problems, wind turbines also harvest natural flows of energy carried by air currents, to feed into the grid and thence into the heating of water in my kettle. However, rather than tapping into sunlight falling to Earth in primordial swamp forests, they convert energy in the here and now from the mass flow of gases in the atmosphere. This movement and its associated energy also ultimately derive

---

[13] NBC News. (2004). *Deadly Power Plants?* Study Fuels Debate: Thousands of Early Deaths Tied to Emissions. (http://www.nbcnews.com/id/5174391/#.U_3fCONdWSo, accessed 26 May 2020.)

[14] Health and Environment Alliance. (2013). The Unpaid Health Bill – How Coal Power Plants Make Us Sick. (https://www.env-health.org/IMG/pdf/heal_report_the_unpaid_health_bill_how_coal_power_plants_make_us_sick_final.pdf, accessed 26 May 2020.)

from the sun, resulting from differential degrees of heating between the poles and the equator, modified by the rotation of the Earth.

Also, of course, the metals from which wind turbines and associated cables and other engineered structures are made are also mined from the Earth's crust, where they have been deposited by natural sedimentation, biological and other processes over geological timescales. So not only are these metals part of the natural world, but nature has played a major hand in concentrating the ores. So, the turbines and gears, transformers and cables, including the wires that lead into my house and the metallic part of the kettle itself, are all a product of nature though manipulated by human ingenuity into a form that serves our convenience.

We could go on to consider the lubricants, coolants, plastics and other substances used in the turbines, all derived from fossil deposits of ancient life since deposited in the Earth's crust as oil and now extracted and modified by human craft.

Nuclear power makes a more modest contribution to the energy mix running through the part of the National Grid that feeds my house. This too, for all the issues associated with its use, is a direct product of nature. The energy itself is released by the fission (splitting) of the nuclei of heavy, radioactive elements sourced by the mining of uranium ores from the Earth's crust. Uranium is not, in fact, a rare element in nature, a constituent of most rocks, dirt and oceanic waters in concentrations roughly about 40 times greater than those of silver.[15] However, to become useful as nuclear fuel, uranium has to be enriched (concentrated), and is then manufactured into rods that allow the fission process to be controlled in nuclear reactors. This is energy derived from the atomic structure of the Earth.

This energy mix is a historical legacy as well as, given where we are today, a pragmatic necessity, as this mix of sources can be increased or decreased controllably to match fluctuating demand as well as variability in the wind and hence turbine-generated sources. The more we can do to reduce the demands we make on the damaging sources and the quicker we shift to renewable sources, the better. That does include reducing the amount of energy we use. This is why my family's investment in solar panels on the roof of our house, to harvest natural energy flows arriving directly as visible light from the sun, adds to the overall energy mix, a contribution that makes sense in terms of avoiding all of those climate change impacts stemming from releasing formerly fossilised carbon and the disinterment of radioactive materials that then have to be stored over geological timescales.

A COMPLEX BREW

So, the biochemical constituents, water and heat of my tea are integral parts of nature, as are their supply chains. I take my tea black and unsweetened. However, milk too clearly derives from nature, the product of cows selectively bred from natural genetic auroch stock, grazed or feed lot fed on vegetation grown from the richness of the soil, augmented often by mined fertiliser, and fused by the

---

[15] Energy Information Administration. (2010). *Summary Status for the US*. (http://www.eia.gov/electricity/, accessed 26 May 2020.)

photosynthetic capture of solar energy. So too the sugar that some people prefer, the sun's rays condensed by sugar cane or beet plants into the chemical bonds that hold these sweet-tasting molecules together.

We could go on to consider the clay mined from the Earth and used to form the mug, the pottery glaze derived originally from a mix of soda and the top layer of silica in clay fired at high temperature to fuse as a glass-like substance, and the energy used to fire it and transport is to the retailer and from the shop to home. We could look at the flows of nature in the water used to wash the cup up too, as indeed the microbial processes in wastewater treatment plants that break down contaminants into simpler products more benign to nature. However, the point has, I think, been made. My cup of tea is inextricably a part of nature.

And when the tea is drunk, and the cup is eventually broken, both will return to nature to be reincorporated (with a little help from biologically driven technology) into nature's structures and cycles. Perhaps some of it will return to me as more tea, those elaborate and biologically active molecules synthesised by the play of sunlight on the leaves of the *Camellia sinensis* plant in some foreign land and culture, as I pause for another reflective moment in years to come?

3 My Trendy Tee-Shirts

Today, I rolled out of bed and made my traditional choice of upper body garment for the day ahead. Basically, this entailed grabbing the top tee-shirt from a tottering pile on my shelf in the bedroom cupboard.

To be brutally honest, I am not a fashion icon. Many of my tee-shirts are 20 years old with a few a good bit longer in the tooth (if shirts had teeth) even than that, though there are a few relative youngsters dotted down the pile that I have since picked up as prizes or been given as presents. However, all are reassuringly 'lived in', varying only on that score by degree. Brand and shiny newness don't exactly rock my world, so that is of no great personal concern as, like me, my tee-shirts have become a bit less than perfectly shaped with the passing of time. I just feel comfortable in them no matter how faded they may be, or how many holes they may have.

Like my aversion to washing the car (a pointless pursuit when one lives in an agricultural landscape with narrow lanes generously coated with agricultural detritus), my inherent scruffiness and disinclination to replace what ain't fundamentally broken also chimes with my wish to avoid wasting resources. "Reduce, reuse, recycle" is best considered as an afterthought to the often-missed "Avoid".

COTTONING ON

A cotton tee-shirt is such an everyday object that it hardly warrants a second thought. But I live in the west country of England, where the climate does not allow for the frost-free growing needs of cotton plants. So, the primary raw material constituting that pile of tee-shirts has made quite a journey to end up in my cupboard. Let's pause a moment to give it that often overlooked 'second thought'.

Cotton is a product of the Earth. As we know from dandelion 'clocks', the fluff that blows from willow trees in the spring and kapok fibres used as upholstery stuffing and for insulation, many plants produce organic fibres to help spread or cosset their seeds. The familiar soft and fluffy cotton fibres that we encounter so commonly around our homes as cotton wool, or spun into yarn that can be used for sewing or woven into fabric, is produced by plants. Cotton plants comprise a variety of species of the genus *Gossypium*, shrubs of the mallow family (Malvaceae) that occur naturally across tropical and subtropical regions from the Americas through to Africa, India and Australia. Cotton fibres grow within a boll — a protective capsule in which the seeds mature — playing a role in dispersing the seeds as the boll opens at maturity.

The use of cotton has a venerable and remarkably widespread legacy. It would appear that cotton was brought into cultivation independently in both the Old World and the New World in prehistoric times, fragments of cotton fabric dated at around 5000 BC found in archaeological remains in both Mexico[1] and the Indus Valley.[2] Cotton has been widely used by humanity for a variety of purposes since that time, with people spreading the plant across the globe as they appropriated and converted land to support their needs and demands. Cotton growing, spinning and dying enjoys centuries of heritage from North Africa and across Asia and the Americas and southern Europe, with significant exports to other nations such as those of northern Europe from the late mediaeval period, as it was not until the Wars of Alexander the Great that the Greeks and the Arabs encountered cotton.

THE POLITICS OF COTTON

Cotton also has significant political contexts beyond those entailed in multinational trade. As one example, under colonial rule during the late 18th and early 19th centuries, the British East India Company oversaw the decline of India's once burgeoning cotton-processing sector through aggressive policies forcing Indian

---

[1] Huckell, L.W. (1993). Plant remains from the Pinaleño Cotton Cache, Arizona. *Kiva. Journal of Southwest Anthropology and History*, 59(2), pp. 147–203.

[2] Moulherat, C., Tengberg, M., Haquet, J.F. and Mille, B. (2002). First evidence of cotton at Neolithic Mehrgarh, Pakistan: Analysis of mineralized fibres from a copper bead. *Journal of Archaeological Science*, 29(12), pp. 1393–1401.

markets to supply only raw cotton and to purchase manufactured textiles from Britain where cotton fabric manufacture emerged as a leading export during the Industrial Revolution. This trade was to exhaust supplies from India, leading British traders to turn to cotton from plantations in the United States and the Caribbean.

This led to 'king cotton' becoming the backbone of the southern American economy by the mid-19th century, earning it further questionable ethical credential as it became the leading occupation amongst slaves. With the advent of the American Civil War, the political significance of cotton emerged once again as the Confederate government cut exports in the hope of forcing Britain to recognise the Confederacy or to enter the war.

Moving ahead to the middle 20th century, Mohandas Gandhi used the inequities of the cotton supply chain, originating in the fields of India where local labourers were remunerated pitifully to supply raw fibres that would eventually feed a lucrative trade clothing remote kings and landlords. This analysis shaped part of Gandhi's expanding nonviolent campaign including the *swadeshi* policy, boycotting foreign-made goods and especially those made in Britain, including his advocacy that *khadi* (homespun cloth) should be worn by Indians instead of British-made textiles. To further this campaign, Gandhi even invented a portable spinning wheel that could be folded down into the size of a small typewriter.[3] The *charkha*, or spinning wheel, was the physical embodiment and symbol of Gandhi's constructive programme. The tri-coloured Indian flag adopted on 22nd July 1947, after India became independent from Great Britain, has in its centre a blue wheel with 24 spokes, this *Dharma Chakra* ('Wheel of Law') represents the continuing progress of the nation and the importance of justice in life though it is often considered also to reflect Gandhi's *charkha*.

BIG BUSINESS; BIG CONSEQUENCES

Cotton remains important as a basis for trade, supporting a variety of uses. Annual global production of cotton today stands at around 25 million tonnes, or 110 million bales (the term used more generally in cotton trading where a bale comprises approximately 0.48 cubic metres, or 17 cubic feet, and weighs 226.8 kilograms, or 500 lb). Cotton represents nearly half the fibre used to make clothes and other textiles worldwide, with much of the rest coming from synthetic products.[4] China is the world's largest producer of cotton, mainly serving its internal market, followed by India and the United States. Other significant producers (in declining order) include Pakistan, Brazil, Uzbekistan, several countries in West Africa, Turkey, Australia, Turkmenistan and Argentina.

All of this cotton is produced from 2.5% of the world's arable land, so the impact of the global trade in cotton is far from slight. It is also a water-intensive crop, requiring more than 20,000 litres of water to produce a kilogramme of cotton

---

[3] Popular Science. (1931). Gandhi Invents Spinning Wheel. *Popular Science* (Bonnier Corporation): 60.
[4] Worldwide Fund for Nature. (2003). *Thirsty Crops*. Worldwide Fund for Nature. (https://www.worldwildlife.org/publications/thirsty-crops-our-food-and-clothes-eating-up-nature-and-wearing-out-the-environment, accessed 26 May 2020.)

(equivalent to a single tee-shirt and pair of jeans), about 73% of the global cotton harvest coming from irrigated land.[5] In some places, diversion or annexation of water to service the cotton trade has been disastrous.

As one striking example, the Aral Sea spanned 67,300 km^2 in the 1950s when it was the world's fourth largest inland sea. The Aral Sea was a rich fishery, supporting a huge Soviet cannery industry on the shoreline in the 1960s. A cotton industry had been present for decades in the basins of the Syr Darya and Amu Darya rivers that fed the Aral Sea. The two countries sharing its coastline, Kazakhstan and Uzbekistan, were at that time part of the Soviet Union. In the 1960s, Soviet engineers embarked on a massive programme of damming and water transfer including a channel 500 kilometres long taking one-third of the water in the rivers to flood rice fields and irrigate cotton fields — both water-intensive crops — constructed in the vast arid steppes surrounding the lake with the objective of increasing agricultural productivity. Thriving fisheries and cotton intensification proved to be far from mutually compatible. By 1980, engineers began to realise that water inflows to the Aral Sea had declined to only 10% of rates recorded in 1960. Aralsk City harbour lost its water in 1970, urban inhabitants observing the day-by-day retreat of the shoreline. The Aral Sea was to become infamous for the abandoned and rusting hulks of large trawlers and container ships stranded in sandy wastelands remote from any residual water, for example, featuring as scenes in the 1977 movie *Close Encounters of the Third Kind*. The last of these trawlers was abandoned with the canneries in 1984 as the Aral Sea receded, starved of fresh water and dried up by the tropical sun. By 1989, this formerly massive water body had split in two small, hyper-saline seas, now known as the North Aral Sea and the South Aral Sea. By 2003, Aralsk City stood not as it once did on the northern seashore but separated from it by 64 kilometres (40 miles) of unproductive salt pan. Large sectors of the local human population were no longer able to access drinking water, any remaining resources highly polluted by fertilisers and pesticides used in cotton farming. The shrinking Aral Sea also lost its capacity to regulate the climate, resulting in more extreme winter and summer weather. Dust storms plagued coastal regions, dry winds whipping up the desiccated former sea bed into salty sand clouds laced with toxic loads of pesticides accumulated from inputs to cotton farming in the feeder rivers. Severe health impacts blighted local communities, including a child mortality rate of 7.5% mainly accounted for by respiratory diseases. Salt and dust were transported up to 200 kilometres away, depressing agricultural productivity in large farming areas in Uzbekistan, Kirghizstan and Turkmenistan. Documentation of the environmental disaster and its terrible humanitarian consequences were conveyed to international audiences in the 2009 film *Aral, the Lost Sea* by Isabel Coixet, at a time when the area of the Aral Sea had already halved and volume had declined to a quarter. Were the decline to continue, this formerly vast and productive inland water body would have vanished entirely in a few years.

---

[5] Worldwide Fund for Nature. (2000). *The Impact of Cotton on Fresh Water Resources and Ecosystems*. Worldwide Fund for Nature. (http://wwf.panda.org/?3686/The-impact-of-cotton-on-fresh-water-resources-and-ecosystems, accessed 26 May 2020.)

However, this may be a story with a potentially better, if far from perfect, ending if current commitments continue to be honoured. There are initial encouraging signs that, following Kazakhstan and Uzbekistan gaining independence from the Soviet Union in 1991, a reversal in policy may be allowing at least part of the Aral Sea slowly to recover. In part, this is driven by another adverse consequence of irrigation, as many fields irrigated under the high evaporation rates of the arid landscape became unproductive variously due to waterlogging or salt panning. The ecology and associated livelihoods of the Aral Sea, like any receiving water body, is intimately linked to the ecology of the landscape in which it is located, and this wider landscape ecology is in turn interdependent with the wider 'environment' of political pressures and economic activities. Economic pressures driving agricultural intensification in the river catchments serving the Aral Sea, under a flawed if potentially well-intentioned model of 'development', had formerly overlooked consequences for collateral impacts on the structure and functioning of the wider ecosystem and the many livelihood needs that it supported. Ultimately, this served only to desiccate and poison this formerly rich and productive inland sea. Attempts to restore the Aral Sea started in 1996 when a dam was built to retain water from the Syr Darya, the river that flows into the north of the Aral Sea, with the aim of regulating the water level in this area of the lake and irrigating the surrounding land. However, this rudimentary dam broke after just a few years. International consternation at the scale of this ecological and humanitarian disaster was a principal factor behind involvement of the United Nations Development Program (UNDP) and approval of an $80m initiative by the World Bank to begin to restore the North Aral Sea. This programme entailed improvements to management of the Syr Darya waters but also, more contentiously, construction in 2004 of a 13 kilometre dam across the isthmus formerly linking the North and South basins of the sea. Results were dramatic, the level of the North Aral Sea increasing by 4 metres after six months. After ten years, the level of the North Aral Sea had risen by 6 metres, its volume had grown by 68% and the Sea's margin had encroached by kilometres over former seabed with salinity also reducing to levels seen prior to 1960 enabling fish populations and other wildlife to return. Local people adjacent to the North Aral Sea have been relieved of the most abject poverty, their disease burdens also lightening and a degree of fishing had resumed though many large former trawlers and tankers remained only as rusted wrecks or had been broken up for scrap. The former seaside city of Aralsk still remained 25 kilometres (nearly 16 miles) from the seashore, though ten years previously this distance had been 75 kilometres (nearly 47 miles). Controversially, these desperate measures have effectively sacrificed the South Aral Sea, which continues not only to lack effective solutions but to be increasingly vulnerable to climate change. Furthermore, many of the factors that triggered the disaster still exist, including production of cotton at substantial environmental and social cost. Challenges remain, though the president of Uzbekistan has called for efforts to attract further international investments to rebuild a green economy founded on energy and water efficient, environmentally friendly technologies. All of this drama to serve the demands of a cotton-hungry world.

In Australia too, the Murray-Darling river basin (1,061,469 square kilometres or 409,654 square miles encompassing about 14% of Australia's land area) contains over 40% of all Australian farms, which produce wool, cotton, wheat, sheep, cattle, dairy produce, rice, oilseed, wine, fruit and vegetables for both domestic and overseas markets.[6] Here too, abstraction of water and heavy inputs of pesticides to support the cotton industry have formerly been heavily implicated in potentially grave impacts on the river, including rising salinity and pesticide content, declining flows, loss of native fishes and other groups of organisms, and a range of other problems.

Globally, agriculture is the largest source of pollution in most countries, with cotton grown around the world accounting for 24% and 11% of the global sales of insecticides and pesticides respectively.[7] However, progress is being made tackling some of this nexus of environmental and ethical issues, for example under the Better Cotton Initiative[8] and also via a renewed focus on protection of bees and other pollinators essential for the setting of cotton crops.[9] So, cotton production is hardly without environmental concerns, which manifest differentially between nations and different supply chains, though I do have to restrain myself for turning this unfamiliar reflection on the ecology of everyday things into a rather more familiar environmentalist call to action!

RETURNING TO NATURE ... OR NOT

As a natural fibre, cotton can be composted at end-of-life to return its constituents into productive uses. Arguably, many of my tee-shirts have already substantially reached that stage in their extended lives, probably long ago exceeding manufacturer expectations.

However, my tee-shirts are familiar and therefore comforting, not just physically but also emotionally. In fact, a common or garden tee-shirt carries with it more than just the fluffy residue of a long-dead seed packaging of a plant and the environmental and social footprints entailed in turning it into a useful product, in addition to the graphics and words printed upon it. It is also as indelibly imprinted with the emotional history and associations of the wearer.

So, my tatty old tee-shirts not only affirm my inherent scruffiness and the ethos of extended product life to minimise overall 'environmental footprint' that I seek to espouse. They clothe me in a breadth of ecological, evolutionary and economic linkages, but have also become 'cloaks of many colours' encoding a life lived within their cottony embrace.

---

[6] http://www.murrayriver.com.au/about-the-murray/murray-darling-basin/ (accessed 26 May 2020).

[7] Worldwide Fund for Nature. (2000). *The Impact of Cotton on Fresh Water Resources and Ecosystems.* Worldwide Fund for Nature. (http://wwf.panda.org/?3686/The-impact-of-cotton-on-fresh-water-resources-and-ecosystems, accessed 26 May 2020.)

[8] http://bettercotton.org/, accessed 26 May 2020.

[9] FAO. (2018). *Why Bees Matter: The Importance of Bees and Other Pollinators for Food and Agriculture.* Food and Agriculture Organization (FAO), Rome. (http://www.fao.org/3/i9527en/i9527en.pdf, accessed 26 May 2020.)

4 Yesterday's Papers

At home, we get one newspaper a week, in the often-vain hope of finding time over the weekend to read it. We used to keep the television guide for the week ahead but, owing to the miracles of the internet, the television is mainly now put on when we want to call up an online programme. But the paper is also useful in precious spare moments over a cup of tea to do their Sudoku puzzles. In this regard, we are not much different to most of the population. We've all probably got a newspaper or two lurking on the coffee table (why do we call them 'coffee tables' when tea is overwhelmingly Britain's and the world's favourite beverage?) or tucked away in a dark recess. We might acquire a newspaper daily or weekly, pick one up sporadically on train journeys, or have one or more freebies posted through the letterbox. We might keep a few back from the recycler for use as firelighters, or to intercept drips from DIY jobs.

A newspaper is such an everyday thing, so cheap in real terms if not entirely free, that we may give it no second thought. So, let's just pause again for a moment to give ourselves some mental space for that second thought.

NATURE IN OUR HANDS

The vast bulk of what we hold in our hands as we read a newspaper is wood pulp. Obviously, trees are the ultimate source of wood fibre, even if it has been on a recycling route to reach us in this form. But its points of origin and stewardship have changed massively over time.

Paper was yet another invention of the ancient Chinese, during the Han Dynasty somewhere around the year 105 AD. The inventor of paper-making is generally thought to be Cai Lun, a court official, said to have been inspired by the nests of wasps and bees. However, archaeological finds from north-east China in around 8 BC suggest that the origins of paper may be earlier than that. Early Chinese paper-makers used cloth rags, tree bark, remnants of hemp, fishing nets and other plant fibre.

The subsequent history of paper-making is hard to track definitively, but it appears to have spread westwards along the Silk Road. It was brought to Europe in the 10th century with Muslims on the Iberian Peninsula and Sicily, spreading progressively throughout much of the rest of Europe by 1400. Writing media in use in Europe before this time included parchment, palm leaves and vellum, as well as papyrus from which the world 'paper' derives. In China, writing was generally on bone, bamboo or silk before the invention of paper. Archaeological evidence indicates that a similar bark-paper writing material was used by Mayans around the 5th century AD.[1] However, materials made from pounded reeds and bark are technically not true paper, which is made from wood pulp, rags and the fibre of other plants including their cellulose context.

One of the more important subsequent innovations in paper-making occurred in mediaeval Europe with mechanisation using water power, the first such mill constructed in the city of Leiria, Portugal, in 1411, and as well as some other mechanised paper-making processes.[2]

Prior to the mechanisation and industrialisation of paper-making, the most common fibre source was from used rags which were themselves derived from hemp, linen and cotton.[3] However, industrialisation marked a transition to using wood pulp from 1843, breaking dependence on recycled materials collected by rag-pickers.

Paper serves many other human needs, ranging from a medium for writing and art, for wrapping, padding for delicate objects, decoration, cleansing for example as toilet papers and tissues, for building products in thicker card as well as paper form, for insulation, for advertising, as money and many other uses besides. And, of course, paper is a common medium for printing.

READING THE PAPERS

The invention of the printing press and the beginning of the Printing Revolution in the 15th century was to serve as a subsequent major spur to European paper production.[4] It is through printing that paper found perhaps its greatest amongst many contributions to societal development for, via the mass and unprecedentedly cheap transfer of characters and images, the portable medium of paper became a profound agent of change across not only Europe but progressively the whole global civilised world.

Knowledge formerly held closely by an educated and otherwise privileged minority became progressively more accessible to the masses, with European book output rising from a few million to around one billion copies within a span of less than four centuries.[5] Continuing declines in unit costs led to the production of the

---

[1] Tobin, T.J. (undated). *The Construction of the Codex in Classic- and Postclassic Period Maya Civilization.* (http://www.mathcs.duq.edu/~tobin/maya/, accessed 26 May 2020.)

[2] Burns, R.I. (1996). Paper comes to the West, 800–1400. In Lindgren, Uta, *Europäische Technik im Mittelalter. 800 bis 1400. Tradition und Innovation* (4th ed.), Berlin: Gebr. Mann Verlag, pp. 413–422.

[3] Göttsching, L. and Pakarinen, H. (2000). Recycled fiber and deinking. *Papermaking Science and Technology*, 7, Finland: Fapet Oy, pp. 12–14.

[4] Burns, R.I. (1996). Paper comes to the West, 800–1400. In Lindgren, Uta, *Europäische Technik im Mittelalter. 800 bis 1400. Tradition und Innovation* (4th ed.), Berlin: Gebr. Mann Verlag, pp. 413–422.

[5] Zeigler, J. (1997). Gutenberg, the Scriptoria, and Websites. *Journal of Scholarly Publishing*, 29(1), p. 36.

first newspapers and pamphlets, further disseminating, for the first time, up-to-date news and novel ideas to more and more strata of society.[6] Thus, the humble piece of paper and the printed words upon it, of which the newspaper was a logical evolutionary step, became a medium for mass awareness, and the transfer of knowledge, doctrine, propaganda and entertainment. Thus, printing spurred the development of communities of common interest, including collaborating scientists, philosophers and politicians, all of whom could now readily communicate their discoveries, thoughts and perspectives one to another and to a wider populace formerly kept in the dark and under the control of an oligarchy formerly empowered by limited access to literacy and recorded wisdoms. Printing and the cheap medium of paper formed important elements in the democratisation of knowledge, quietly ushering in a profound knowledge revolution across society. Much more could be said about the technological progress of printing and its influence on societal evolution, but this very brief summary is enough to reveal how profound and potentially subversive a device the simple and familiar old newspaper has been to the unfolding of cultural progress.

THE WOOD FIBRE FOR THE TREES

Today, as for much of recent history, a wide variety of types of paper are made predominantly from wood fibre, some finer papers also including cotton or silk fibres. This wood fibre is derived either from hardwood or softwood trees. Hardwood trees tend to produce short, dense fibres delivering strength, whereas softwood trees comprise longer, softer fibres providing bulk. Differing combinations of fibre are used to produce a diversity of types of paper.

Global production of paper and cardboard in 2017 was approximately 419.7 million metric tonnes, more than half of this comprising packaging paper and almost one-third was attributable to graphic paper, with China, the United States and Japan accounting for more than half of global paper production.[7] All of this, of course exerts a substantial demand on forest resources, with a substantial amount of wood fibre traded internationally. Many countries, such as the UK that has a reasonably significant forest resource (13% of total UK land area comprised woodland in 2019), nevertheless meet the vast bulk of their wood fibre demands from international markets rather than domestic sources. Wood fibre used for paper derives from three principal sources: fresh fibres sourced from natural forests; fibre derived from tree plantations; or recycled sources including by-products from industrial or post-consumer waste. Inputs of fresh wood fibre are required in recycling processes as fibre quality degrades with each cycle, fibres typically becoming degraded and unusable after five to seven cycles, as well as to make up for losses through non-recoverable paper items such as medical applications and domestic tissues.

---

[6] Weber, J. (2006), Strassburg, 1605: The origins of the newspaper in Europe. *German History*, 24(3), pp. 387–412.

[7] Garside, M. (2019). *Paper Industry — Statistics & Facts. Statista*, 22nd November 2019. (https://www.statista.com/topics/1701/paper-industry/, accessed 7 June 2020.)

The Earth's dwindling coverage of old-growth forests is a precious resource. The ecological complexity and biodiversity values of forest systems co-evolved over millennia cannot simply be replaced. These complex forest ecosystems also support indigenous communities and traditional livelihoods, as well as playing important roles in preventing soil erosion, storing substantial carbon contributing significantly to global climate regulation and influencing weather systems such as the vast jungles of the Congo Basin that generate as much as 90% of the rain that falls back into the forest in a close cycle. Loss or degradation of these residual natural forests can be disastrous for many ecological, economic and societal reasons, and with global ramifications. We can add to this the contribution of forest and wider ecosystem degradation to reductions of natural barriers to novel diseases crossing over from animals to humans.[8] Liquidating this precious resource for short-term revenue generation through extraction of timber and wood fibre is therefore very unwise, and measures are in place globally to halt forest destruction for these and other utilitarian purposes.

Tree plantations for wood fibre production cannot be compared favourably with natural forest. Essentially, they constitute a crop, lacking the ecological complexity and range of human benefits provided by natural forest ecosystems. However, they can be efficient means to produce virgin wood fibre, reducing impacts on more natural forest systems. They may also be lucrative. With best forest management programmes — a complex topic well beyond the scope of this book — they can also be beneficial, or at least of minimal decrement, to wildlife, local and equitable economies, landscape stability and water resource protection.

Many types of newsprint, as toilet paper and facial tissue, are essentially a low grade of paper. Consequently, they are most commonly produced from recycled and deinked pulp from recycled sources in industrialised countries.

THE CYCLIC NATURE OF PAPER

So, what exactly is it that you hold in your hands as you read a newspaper, or perhaps even read this book if you are not reading it on an electronic device? You may not have thought about it this way before, but you are holding the product of photosynthesis. The cellulose fibre comprising the bulk of paper, as indeed the cotton tee-shirts considered in another chapter, is fused by the alchemy that occurs in chloroplasts in plant cells which use energy captured from sunlight to incorporate carbon dioxide and water into complex sugar molecules. And, of course, when paper is burned, all of that energy captured from sunshine is released again as the chemical bonds in complex molecules are broken down.

There is much more ecology in the everyday newspaper, ranging from the substantial use of water in industrial paper-making processes, fillers which comprise inert chemicals filling the open structure between paper fibres (glossy coated paper

---

[8] Everard, M., Johnston, P., Santillo, D. and Staddon, C. (2020). The role of ecosystems in mitigation and management of Covid-19 and other zoonoses. *Environmental Science and Policy*, 111, pp. 7–17. DOI: https://doi.org/10.1016/j.envsci.2020.05.017.

can comprise as much as 20% by weight of clay), optical brighteners, and a variety of other more exotic chemicals used in paper-making and the printing process.

However, in thinking of the ecology of this everyday object, there are pronounced similarities between newspapers and mayflies, or perhaps leaves. A strange analogy perhaps, but mayflies, butterflies and leaves are ephemeral forms within longer life cycles. Newspapers too, like many printed paper products, are ephemeral manifestations of matter and energy in a useful form with an often-limited lifetime. The newspaper in your hands is little more than a temporary form, assembled from natural chemicals and energy albeit in this case re-engineered by technological ingenuity rather than biological evolution, to serve a particular function at a particular moment in time.

Few paper products enjoy long lives. Some paper-based books defy this generality; some are now over a millennium old. However, most printed paper and many other paper products have only limited lives. Newspapers are one such product that transitions into waste almost within hours of production.

It is consequently vital that newspapers are produced in such a way that they are readily recyclable, recovering valuable resources for further productive uses and avoiding the accumulation of waste. Today, it takes just seven days for a recycled newspaper to come back as a newspaper again in the UK, where 79% of paper and cardboard is recovered for recycling,[9] representing a saving of 13 million tonnes of CO_2 equivalent emissions (the equivalent of taking over million cars off the road). Newsprint used in the UK contains around 78% of recycled paper, and corrugated packaging material comprises nearly 100% recycled material.

Paper and cardboard were the most recycled materials in 2017 at 79%.

So, a newspaper is one of modern society's more successful innovations. It is so because the sheer power of the medium for the exchange of knowledge and cross-fertilisation of minds is vastly underappreciated, albeit arguably used by sizeable majority today largely for the most trivial aspects of its potential. But the societal life cycle of a newspaper is also amazingly successful in emulating nature's production systems such that, when its immediate purpose has been served, it may be re-assimilated benignly by human-aided, nature-emulating cyclic systems.

---

[9] BBC. (2019). *Where Does Recycling and Rubbish from the UK Go? BBC News: Science & Environment,* 31 September 2019. (https://www.bbc.co.uk/news/science-environment-49827945, accessed 26 May 2020.)

5 A Simple Bowl of Rice

During his term as British Foreign Secretary in April 2001, the late Robin Cook memorably gave what came to be known as the 'chicken tikka masala' speech. Cook's point was that chicken tikka masala had become a true British national dish. In part, this reflected a transition over a generation from fish and chips as the great British staple takeaway meal towards a far greater volume of curries. Chicken tikka masala lacks any authentic Indian or Bangladeshi roots, though chicken tikka itself is a popular Indian dish. The masala sauce was added by adventurous restaurateurs to cater for the desire of British people to have their meat served in tomato-rich (and often luridly coloured) gravy. The key point made by Cook was that chicken tikka masala had not only become the most popular British dish, but that it illustrated the way Britain absorbs and adapts external influences. This, felt Cook, was a near perfect example of how multiculturalism was a positive force for the British economy and society, holding important clues to our understanding of 'Britishness'. However, we should also not overlook the influence of another factor with far more serious ramifications, namely the depletion of marine fisheries with consequent implications for the availability and price of fish.

A MODERN WESTERN STAPLE

The key reason for this ramble through an aspect of Britain's recent culinary history is to highlight how rice has become a staple of the Western diet, regardless of the fact that so little of it is grown in many of its major global developed world market territories. Rice is consumed as part of takeaway meals, in restaurants or cooked at home, as a common constituent of Indian, Chinese and other meals. It is also a key element of risotto and paella from the Mediterranean, and a wide range of other dishes including as a desert in the form for example of rice pudding or rice paper in cakes, 'rice crispies' and other breakfast cereals and snack foods. So, we perhaps have become too familiar with the fact that this exotic grass seed, mainly of Chinese extraction, has become a staple foodstuff of British and many other temperate nations.

We in Britain certainly associate rice strongly with Indian food. Yet I work extensively in India, particularly in arid and semi-arid regions where I work with academics, government and inspiring charitable organisations engaging with local communities to help them better steward their water resources and other supportive ecosystems. In the Thar Desert of northern India's Rajasthan state, being offered a small bowl of rice with a meal is a sign of deep respect. For, familiar as we are with rice as an accompaniment to Indian meals, it is a water-intensive crop that demands much of the limited water resource in the dry lands of Rajasthan. Here, wheat, generally in the form of a chapatti, is the most common accompaniment to a simple meal of dhal, bindi and other locally grown vegetables.

Rice is also as scarce or absent in other places I work in the Indian Himalayas, though this is due to the cooler climate of the uplands rather than primarily related to limitation in the supply of water. Rice plants are not frost-tolerant and so, where cultivated in cooler climates, have to be grown indoors until the risk of frost has passed. All of which illustrates that there may be more to the everyday bowl of rice that we might enjoy mainly unthinkingly as a staple accompaniment to our needs in the temperate West and other industrialised nations.

WHAT IS RICE?

Rice is a type of grass (belonging to the true grass family *Poaceae*), a familiar and ubiquitous group of plants with something like 10,000 species comprising the world's fifth-largest flowering plant family. Grasses are vital components to the character and functioning of planetary ecosystems, with grasslands estimated to comprise 20% of the vegetation cover of the Earth, various species of grass dominant or common in habitats ranging from savannah to tundra, forests and wetlands. The grasses also serve a wide range of human needs, with many species domesticated for grazing, hay, cereals for food and stock feed, biofuels, building materials such as bamboo and thatch, and a range of other uses. Indeed, the domestication of various cereal crops — rice, maize (corn), wheat, barley, oats and millet — has served as a foundation for agriculture, underpinning the settlement and differentiation of civilisations around the world.

Rice grains are basically seeds from two species of wetland grasses, *Oryza sativa* (Asian rice) and *Oryza glaberrima* (African rice). Of these, Asian rice is the dominant crop grown for subsistence and commercial purposes globally, with many cultivated strains across two principal sub-species: the sticky, short-grained variety (*japonica* or *sinica*); and the non-sticky, long-grained variety (*indica*). Optimal cultivation of these strains varies, with *japonica* usually cultivated in dry fields in temperate East Asia, upland areas of Southeast Asia and high elevations in South Asia. *Indica* varieties are mainly grown semi-submerged in water in lowlands throughout tropical Asia and many other parts of the world. It was initially thought that Asian rice was first brought into cultivation in the Yangtze Valley of China somewhere between 9,000 to 10,000 years ago. However, subsequent genetic evidence has found that all forms of Asian rice result from a single domestication of a wild rice species (*Oryza rufipogon*) somewhere between 8,200 and 13,500 years ago, also in China.[1] From here, rice domestication spread by multiple separate routes throughout Asia, Oceania and Africa.[2] Wherever rice has been transported by people, it has contributed to their ability to feed themselves, and its stewardship has often also defined their cultures.

By contrast, African rice is believed to have been domesticated 2,000–3,000 years ago from a wild African ancestor, *Oryza barthii*, in the inland delta of the Upper Niger River in modern day Mali, West Africa.[3] African rice is today a staple food throughout West Africa, and is also prized for its delicate, nutty taste. It grows best in the alluvial soils that remain the principal habitat of its progenitor wild species, and it is also more resilient than Asian rice in its growing requirements in terms of fluctuations in water level, iron toxicity, soil infertility, severe climatic conditions and human neglect. African rice also shows better resistance to a range of pests, diseases and parasitic plants. However, African rice grains are also more brittle than Asian rice and have lower yield in optimal conditions, so it is of far lower importance as a commercial crop.

Today, rice is the most widely consumed staple food globally, a major part in the diet of more than half the world's population especially in Asia where most of it is grown for local consumption. The importance of rice has been recognised for many centuries, for example in India where it was once known as *dhanya* meaning 'the sustainer of the human race'.[4] Globally, rice is the grain with the second-highest worldwide production after maize (generally referred to as 'corn' in the United States though that term has more generic applicability to cereals in the UK). Maize, rice and wheat collectively provide 48% of total calories and also 42% of total protein exceeding that of meat, fish, milk and eggs combined to people in the developing world comprising over half of global population.[5] Rice is grown in more than a hundred countries, with a total harvested area of approximately 158 million hectares, producing more than 700 million tons annually (of which 470 million tons is milled rice).[6]

---

[1] Molina, J., Sikora, M., Garud, N., Flowers, J. M., Rubinstein, S., Reynolds, A., Huang, P., Jackson, S., Schaal, B. A., Bustamante, C. D., Boyko, A. R. and Purugganan, M.D. (2011). Molecular evidence for a single evolutionary origin of domesticated rice. *Proceedings of the National Academy of Sciences*, 108(20), p. 8351.

[2] Bellwood, P. (2011). The checkered prehistory of rice movement southwards as a domesticated cereal—from the Yangzi to the equator. *Rice*, 4(3), pp. 93–103.

[3] Linares, O.F. (2002). African rice (*Oryza glaberrima*): History and future potential. *Proceedings of the National Academy of Sciences of the United States of America*, 99(25), pp. 16360–16365.

[4] https://www.buddhaglobal.com/wpcproduct/rice/, accessed 26 May 2020.

[5] Kropff, M. and Morell, M. (Undated). *The Cereals Imperative of Future Food Systems*, International Rice Research Institute (IRRI). (https://www.irri.org/news-and-events/news/cereals-imperative-future-food-systems, accessed 26 May 2020.)

[6] Ricepedia. (Undated). *Rice Productivity*. Ricepedia, a project of CGIAR. (http://ricepedia.org/rice-as-a-crop/rice-productivity, accessed 26 May 2020.)

RICE AS A MEDICINE

However, rice is far more than just a food. As noted when considering *Reading the Tea Leaves*, the complex biochemistry that plants have evolved throughout millennia imbues them with a variety of biochemically active constituents, some of which have been exploited by humanity. The seed also has a long history in traditional medicine, particularly in products derived from brown rice and also rice oil produced from rice bran, some of its traditional uses endorsed by modern scientific studies.[7] One common medicinal application is in the treatment of skin conditions, generally in the form of a paste of boiled rice that is applied to boils, sores, swellings and skin blemishes, sometimes with the addition of other herbs to increase their medicinal effects. Rice boiled into a glutinous consistency is also often used to treat stomach upsets, heartburn and indigestion.

Extracts from brown rice have also been used to treat breast cancer, stomach cancer and warts, as well as indigestion, nausea and diarrhoea. A broth of boiled rice has been used since antiquity as an antidiarrheal agent, and the rich starch content of rice water has antigastritic and demulcent (protective of internal mucous membranes and also of the skin) qualities that suit it for the treatment of pancreatitis, gastritis and stomach ache, and it has also been long used in Indian ayurvedic medicine to fight diarrhoea, fever, inflammations and painful urination.[8]

At the dawn of the 1980s, I tried the 'macrobiotic' diet, which had become popular at least amongst the alternative culture to which I associated at the time. The pseudoscientific principle of macrobiotics is that all foods comprise yin and yang elements, based loosely on Chinese philosophy, with brown rice representing a perfect balance of the two elements. I ate little else for a few weeks, until a nurse who was a friend pretty much pinned me down and insisted I take some urine tests, which instantly confirmed malnutrition! So, yes, rice has a place in medicine and balanced nutrition, but also in some pseudoscientific approaches to both that served me poorly in my quest for health and enlightenment!

OTHER USES OF RICE

Rice hay is also an important product as stock animal bedding and fodder throughout the dry months in much of India, often stored in characteristic stacks up in trees to avoid the unwanted attentions of wild and domestic animals.

Rice is also the source of laundry starch, can be used as a cleaning agent in cramped spaces (for example adding water and rice grains to scour and swill out the insides of vases), can act as a drying agent for electronic equipment and in salt shakers, may serve as stuffing in soft toys and to weight down a pastry case when it is being baked blind (without filling), can be used to produce non-dairy rice 'milk',

---

[7] Umadevi, M., Pushpa, R., Samapathkumar, K.P. and Bhowmik, D. (2012). Rice — Traditional medicinal plant in India. *Journal of Pharmacognosy and Phytochemistry*, 1(1), pp. 6-12. ISSN 228-4136. (http://www.phytojournal.com/vol1Issue1/Issue_may_2012/1.2.pdf, accessed 26 May 2020.)

[8] Phytotherapy (preparations with rice for the health). (http://www.botanical-online.com/english/medicinalpropertiesrice.htm, accessed 26 May 2020.)

is amenable to use as a skin-washing agent and, owing to its latent heat, it can be used in body-warming applications such as in hot water bottle replacements.[9]

Rice then is just one of very many products of nature's long genetic heritage of plants and other organisms that we have purloined for our use as food, fuel, fibre, fodder, thatching and other building materials, medicine, decoration, comfort and a host of other uses.

RICE AS AN ORGANISING PRINCIPLE IN CULTURES AND LIVELIHOODS

Rice cultivation is also the principal activity and source of income for about 100 million households in Asia and Africa.[10] Across the tropical world, terraced rice paddy systems built to intercept and retain water flows, soil and nutrients characterise many steep slopes. Some, such as the Banaue Rice Terraces in the Philippines, are 2,000 years old, carved by successive generations of local people into the mountain sides. Similar systems are found across the Far East, the Indian sub-continent, some hill slopes of Africa and in some landscapes with similar topography in south America. Built largely by hand, maintained over the centuries by the constant attention and labour of communities shaped by the need to tend these systems for mutual food security, this type of collaborative activity binds communities throughout the tropical world and across time. Human as well as technological infrastructure is vital for the continued functioning and productivity of these paddy systems. Some, such as the Banaue Rice Terraces, are considered wonders of the world, nowadays with considerable modern tourism value. However, all shape communities and li-velihoods, influencing their timings in response to the pulse of monsoons and other weather systems. Often, they also have notable spiritual significance, stemming for the bonding of people around common stewardship of nature's productive capacities.

In Asia, the overwhelming majority of rice is produced within walking distance of where it is eaten[11] using centuries-old traditional knowledge to intercept natural flows of water through landscapes. Though 'low tech' in Western industrial terms, terraced cultivation systems common throughout Asia are remarkably efficient, conserving not only water but also soil and nutrients. In some areas, rice paddy is also used for polyculture, with juvenile fish introduced when the paddy is flooded then harvested for food along with the rice.

In areas such as the hill slopes of the Western Ghats of India, where the upland forest habitat serves a crucial role in the capture and storage of water upon which the river systems and hundreds of millions of people across the otherwise arid Deccan Peninsula depend, water is used so efficiently at local scale that it barely has any impact on catchment hydrology. This sophisticated and well-adapted form of

---

[9] http://www.care2.com/greenliving/13-surprising-uses-for-rice.html#ixzz35qDwKXip, accessed 26 May 2020.

[10] Umadevi, M., Pushpa, R., Samapathkumar, K.P. and Bhowmik, D. (2012). Rice — Traditional medicinal plant in India. *Journal of Pharmacognosy and Phytochemistry*, 1(1), pp. 6-12. ISSN 228-4136. (http://www.phytojournal.com/vol1Issue1/Issue_may_2012/1.2.pdf, accessed 26 May 2020.)

[11] Codrington, S. (2005). *Planet Geography*. Solid Star Press: North Ryde, Australia.

terraced farming is found from Thailand to Java, Bali, India, Cambodia, Sri Lanka, the Philippines and even as far afield as Peru; cultures may come and go, but the paddy system persists.[12] This form of localised communal approach to the tapping of environmental flows of water, both through soils and in the form of capture of rainfall to meet local needs, has underpinned great civilisations upon which empires have been built, even if the most basic yet vital technologies supporting the livelihoods of most of their people have been almost entirely overlooked.

RICE AND SPIRITUALITY

Rice has ritual and ceremonial significance in much of Japanese culture. In traditional sumo, for example, throwing of rice is part of the ritual of this form of martial art imbued with all manner of spiritual meanings. Sumo matches also take place in a dohyō ring made of rice straw bales built on top of a platform made of mixed clay and sand. In wider Japanese culture, sacred gifts of rice to the gods are known as 'goku', the cultivation of this select rice occurring in special places. Another type of sacred rice in Japan is cleansed specially as an offering to grant safe childbirth.

African rice is also used in a ritualistic context, as well as in African traditional medicine. Votive offerings of rice are also commonplace across India, as well as other Asian countries. Elsewhere in the world, rice is also an ingredient in medicines and cosmetics, as well as playing various roles in crafts and religious ceremonies. Rice then is not only a directly consumable product of nature, but one that has bestowed a host of religious, community-building, medicinal and other values upon humanity, and its stewardship has shaped whole societies and landscapes.

A SIMPLE BOWL OF RICE?

In summary, there is nothing 'simple' about a simple bowl of rice. Every grain carries the genetic inheritance of 3.85 billion years of evolution. It is also the product of countless centuries of selective breeding and human stewardship, including part of land uses that have bound cultures throughout millennia, forged from careful stewardship of soils and water flows merged with sunlight in the alchemy of photosynthesis. Rice also arrives to us readily on the back of global trading partnerships of immense value.

With every mouthful of this commonplace staple food, we are absorbing these genetic, political, ecological and economic realities, connecting with nature's beneficence as exactly as we depend on nature to break down and re-assimilate bodily wastes in the production of new resources to support our continuing wellbeing. Nature is everywhere, making, maintaining and mending, including in every molecule of the everyday simple bowl of rice.

There is, in fact, absolutely nothing simple about a bowl of rice. And that is before we think about the bowl itself, and the heat and water used to cook it!

---

[12] Pearce, F. (2004). *Keepers of the Spring: Reclaiming Our Water in an Age of Globalization*. Island Press: Washington, DC.

6 Bath Time

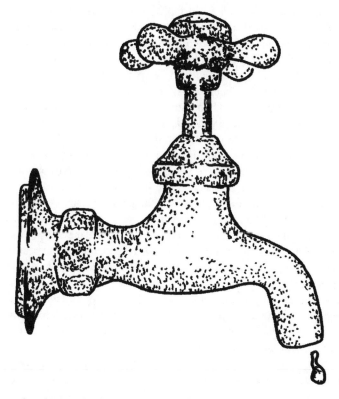

I do not often have a bath. I don't mean by this that I do not wash! Rather, the shower at home is more convenient in a life that seems to be lived rather too much like a pinball in a machine played by a maniac. It is also less demanding of planetary resources, particularly of water and energy. Furthermore, our electric shower bypasses grave inefficiencies in the plumbing system of the 1950s ex-Council house in which we live. So, a bath is a luxury that I reserve for myself intermittently during 'down time' in my all too frequent stays in hotels.

Lying back in a bath of hot water is, therefore, a rare luxury, also serving as a refuge from phones, emails or other digital interruptions, where precious moments of space for reflection can be enjoyed in splendid isolation. Lying back in the bath, thinking about all the ecological connections that we experience through everyday things, naturally led me to thinking about the bath itself.

PLUMBED INTO NATURE

Soporifically buoyed in the warm water, it is easy to conjure quasi-scientific analogies. These may range from speculation about embryonic memories of suspension in warm amniotic fluid, genetic memories of our amphibious progenitors or the claims that humans emerged not as arboreal apes but buoyed by tropical swamp water (as evidenced by our hairlessness, subcutaneous fat and the unlikely scenario of a pregnant woman swinging from bough to bough to evade predators) as part of the 'aquatic ape theory'.[1,2] This is all fascinating, but mainly speculative. But our ecological connections with the bath are far more tangible than that.

The plumbing system — the pipework and taps — are forged from metal mined as ore from the Earth's crust, where it had been lain down and sequestered by natural processes over geological time. Equally, the plastic plug and polymer shell of the bath tub too are parts of nature, modified by the hand of humanity from plant matter sequestered and modified from Carboniferous forests. So, yes, I am as immersed in nature in the bath as I am when swimming in the river or walking in the woods. And that's before we even begin to think about the mysterious fluid surrounding me.

Now, water is an amazing thing. It is the most abundant chemical compound on the Earth's surface, covering 71% of planetary surface area. Not only that, it is also the only common substance that occurs here in the three phases of liquid, solid and gas. It also pervades and plays crucial roles in all environmental media — land, water and air also conveying the fourth element of energy. Water also dissolves many substances, and is therefore often referred to as a universal solvent. Odourless, tasteless, largely colourless (in reality it has just a faint hint of blue) and largely incompressible, fresh water therefore dissolves, dissipates, suspends and otherwise connects the multiple chemical, physical and biological processes comprising the intricate workings of the living Earth system. Much more could be said about the unique properties of water, such as how liquid water is semi-crystalline, about its surface tension properties allowing various bugs and insects too walk on its surface, and how the solid phase of ice is lighter than the liquid phase so can form a surface layer insulating water bodies. However, it is perhaps more informative for our immediate purpose to turn to what water does for life, including for us humans.

THE PLANETARY ORIGINS OF WATER

Much of the water on Earth was present as our home planet formed from a cloud of space dust, progressively condensing into a solid core and outer layers of lower density. The early atmosphere comprised mainly water vapour, carbon dioxide and compounds of sulphur, nitrogen and chlorine, with some molecules of methane and ammonia. This dense soup of atmospheric gases was, therefore, rich in what we refer to today as 'greenhouse gases'. The term 'greenhouse effect' was first coined by Swedish scientist Svante Arrhenius, though was first predicted in 1827 by French mathematician Joseph Fourier. This effect is so named as a range of 'greenhouse gases' absorb infrared radiation, trapping heat within the atmosphere and so elevating temperatures near the Earth's surface through acting much like a glass greenhouse. The result is a rise in the

---

[1] Elaine, M. (1982). *The Aquatic Ape*. Stein and Day Publishers.
[2] Vaneechoutte, M., Kuliukas, A. and Verhaegen, M. (2011). *Was Man More Aquatic in the Past? Fifty Years after Alister Hardy — Waterside Hypotheses of Human Evolution*. Bentham Science Publishers.

temperature of the Earth's atmosphere above that which could be predicted alone from its distance of 93 million miles (nearly 150 milion kilometres) from the sun.

As the early terrestrial atmosphere comprised around 98% carbon dioxide, a potent greenhouse gas, it was much warmer than today, reaching temperatures of as much as 85–110°C. This prevented the formation of large volumes of water in liquid form, with water vapour also acting as a powerful greenhouse gas exacerbating the warming effect. However, as the atmosphere gradually cooled during the Earth's evolution, water was progressively able to condense into clouds and then into liquid form as rains fell on bare rock. And so commenced a water cycle that, over time, produced a covering of soil through the actions both of weathering and emerging life.

Today, this warming process enables the existence of water in its liquid form on this planet, something that would not happen without the greenhouse effect. And the planet's rich water resource came to support the genesis and proliferation of living things, which interact to maintain not only today's balance of greenhouse gases but also the 'ozone layer' in the stratosphere which allowed and continues to allow the proliferation of life in shallower water and on the land surface by blocking damaging levels of ultraviolet radiation from the sun. It is this interdependence of life with the life-sustaining processes of the Earth that led British scientist James Lovelock, along with American evolutionary biologist Lynne Margulis, to promote the now well-known Gaia hypothesis which regards the whole-Earth system as a kind of self-regulating super-organism. Water is essential for all living things. Indeed, it is not too dramatic to state that it is water that makes life possible.

THE PLANETARY WATER WHEEL

Only some 0.001% of the global water resource occurs in the atmosphere.[3] Here, it continues to play a significant role in regulating the planet's temperature as water vapour is the strongest of the common greenhouse gases. Furthermore, in addition to their role in the natural greenhouse effect, the brightness of clouds reflects solar radiation resulting in a net, if variable, cooling effect on the climate system that depends on the height, type and optical properties of the clouds. (This reflectivity is known as 'albedo'.) The water cycle is also a crucial element of weather systems, vectored by the troposphere (the lowest altitude band of the atmosphere).

The water cycle is also amongst the most fundamental of processes shaping the structure of the Earth and its ecosystems. Water-vectored and other weathering processes break down rocks and soils into ever smaller fragments, and eventually to constituent substances. Rainfall absorbs dissolved carbon dioxide from the surrounding air, causing rainwater to be slightly acidic which augments the capacity of water for erosion and dissolution. Released sediment particles and constituent chemical substances then enter into circulation in the biosphere (the living elements of the Earth).

The *hydrosphere*, a term used to define all fresh and saline surface water as well as subterranean groundwater, interacts deeply with the atmosphere, shaping the climate and its more local manifestation as weather. The atmosphere and oceans are

---

[3] https://www.usgs.gov/mission-areas/water-resources/science, accessed 26 May 2020.

particularly strongly coupled through the exchange of water vapour, heat, various gases and other constituents, which contribute to important climatic processes such as evaporation and condensation, cloud formation, precipitation, runoff and energy transfer through weather systems. As one example, 'atmospheric rivers', comprising plumes of concentrated moisture in the atmosphere that may be several thousand kilometres long yet only a few hundred kilometres wide, may be particularly significant for the transport of water vapour over long distances.[4] A large atmospheric river may carry a greater flux of water than the Amazon, the planet's largest river, and atmospheric rivers account for over 90% of global north-south water vapour transport.[5] Atmospheric rivers are becoming increasingly implicated as behind localised serious flooding events.[6,7] Also, somewhere between 50% and 85% of the oxygen content in the air we breathe is produced by oceanic phytoplankton (tiny plants suspended in seawater).[8] Complex interactions between the water cycle, linking all planetary components, constitute a diversity of feedback systems.

SCARE WATER

There is a lot of water on Earth, possibly as much as 1,386,000,000 cubic km (332,500,000 cubic miles).[9] However, for all this abundance, fresh water is a scarce resource as only something like 2.5%[10] or 3.5%[11] of the total global water resource is fresh. Furthermore, around 1.7% of the global water resource (about half of global freshwater) is locked up in ice caps, glaciers and permanent snow, with a further 0.22% locked up as ground ice and permafrost and 0.001% in the form of soil moisture.[12] Furthermore, 0.001% of the global resource is in the atmosphere and 0.0001% is contained by biology. Whilst 0.76% of the global resource

[4] Zhu, Y. and Newell, R.E. (1994). Atmospheric rivers and bombs. *Geophysics Research Letters*, 21(18), pp. 1999–2002.

[5] Zhu, Y. and Newell, R.E. (1998). A proposed algorithm for moisture fluxes from atmospheric rivers. *Monthly Weather Review*, 126(3), pp. 725–735.

[6] Fischetti, M. (2012). Mysterious atmospheric river soaks California, where megaflood may be overdue. *Scientific American*, 30 November 2012. (http://blogs.scientificamerican.com/observations/2012/11/30/mysterious-atmospheric-river/, accessed 26 May 2020.)

[7] Lavers, D.A., *et al.* (2013). Future changes in atmospheric rivers and their implications for winter flooding in Britain. *Environmental Research Letters*, 8, p. 034010 (http://iopscience.iop.org/1748–9326/8/3/034010/article, accessed 26 May 2020.)

[8] EarthSky. (2014). How much do oceans add to world's oxygen? (http://earthsky.org/earth/how-much-do-oceans-add-to-worlds-oxygen, accessed 26 May 2020.)

[9] Gleick, P. H. (1996). Water resources. In *Encyclopedia of Climate and Weather*, ed. by S. H. Schneider, New York: Oxford University Press, vol. 2, pp. 817–823.

[10] Gleick, P. H. (1996). Water resources. In Encyclopedia of Climate and Weather, New York: Oxford University Press, New York, vol. 2, pp. 817–823.

[11] USGS. (Undated). *Ice, Snow, and Glaciers and the Water Cycle.* (https://www.usgs.gov/special-topic/water-science-school/science/ice-snow-and-glaciers-and-water-cycle?qt-science_center_objects=0#qt-science_center_objects, accessed 26 May 2020.)

[12] USGS. (Undated). *Ice, Snow, and Glaciers and the Water Cycle.* (https://www.usgs.gov/special-topic/water-science-school/science/ice-snow-and-glaciers-and-water-cycle?qt-science_center_objects=0#qt-science_center_objects, accessed 26 May 2020.)

comprises fresh groundwater, a substantial proportion of this is deep or otherwise inaccessible. This leaves 0.0008% as swamp water, 0.0002% rivers and 0.007% fresh lakes. Beneath all of these possibly bewildering statistics, it is safe to say that, despite the ubiquity of water, only a minute proportion is available to humanity and this too can be highly localised.

To say that the scarce resource of fresh water is important to humanity is to understate the case massively. Indeed, water makes up 55% to 78% of the human body, depending on age and gender, two-thirds of this bodily water occurring inside our cells and the rest between the cells and in the blood. Of this internal river, we exchange at least 2½ litres (4.4 pints) daily, releasing it back into nature via the moisture we exhale and in sweat, urine and feces, and replacing it with what we drink and eat. This indivisible link makes us as much 'water babies' as creatures of the land.

WATER AND THE EVOLUTION OF CIVILISATIONS

Local climate conditions influencing availability and flows of water determine what food we can harvest and what crops and livestock we can rear, and the character of the landscapes and livelihoods that this makes possible. So, water has played an often-underappreciated hand in shaping cultures and civilisations.

The first recorded global civilisation 9,000 years ago at the city of Uruk in Mesopotamia, a landscape between the Tigris and Euphrates rivers currently encompassed by modern-day Iraq, was substantially a story about the manipulation of water. Harnessing flows of water on to cropped land allowed people to escape the drudgery of a daily hunt for food, thereby enabling settlement and differentiation within society. Control of water has underpinned the progression of successive civilisations, just as misuse of water and the substances dissolved in it has, in many cases, contributed to their collapse.[13] Our continuing dependence on water includes not just its direct use for consumption, washing, cooking and waste disposal and dispersion, but also for transport, defence, energy-harvesting by mills and turbines, irrigation, moisture in soils and forests, cooling, natural fertilisation and regeneration of floodplains, spiritual symbolism, regional character, economic and tourism resources and many more factors besides.

HYDRAULIC CIVILISATIONS

For many of our domestic consumption and disposal needs, simple access to rivers, lakes, wells or disposal pits would have sufficed for low-density human settlements. However, a growing density of humanity attracted to or breeding in such favourable waterscapes brings with it many challenges.

The term 'hydraulic civilization' (its original American spelling) was coined by German—American historian Karl Wittfogel in 1957, an insightful term in an otherwise

---

[13] Diamond, J. (2005). *Collapse: How Societies Choose to Fail or Succeed*. Penguin Books: New York.

rather racially framed book.[14] In essence, the term describes civilisations that have learned to bring water to where they settle, rather than settling where water is immediately available. Modern cities would not be possible without the diversion of water, essential for sourcing of food, energy and other commodities, export of waste materials and many other needs. Booming settlements access increasingly remote 'green' and 'blue' hinterlands beyond the continuously sprawling footprint of burgeoning urban centres. This, of course, includes increasingly remote and large-scale engineering to plumb people into the benefits of direct connection with watercourses.

Techniques to bring clean water into people's homes can entail 'heavy engineering' approaches such as pumped abstraction and treatment of water from rivers and underground, as well as large dams and transfers from adjacent river basins. However, this does not replace natural processes, which contribute the vital underpinning resources and additional 'value add' of natural water storage and purification by catchment processes. Equally, to ensure pollutants do not overwhelm the ecosystems of watercourses into which they are ultimately discharged, humans have made use of natural microbial processes in wastewater treatment technologies, such as trickling filters, activated sludge and constructed wetlands, to reduce loads of potentially problematic substances and pathogens before the release of effluent into receiving water environments, where further natural processes do the final 'polishing' to return the water into a condition that we can use yet again. Enabled by whatever degree of technological sophistication to compensate for our greater population density and localised urbanisation, all of this grand water management technology is purely and simply a means to extend our ability to dip ourselves into nature's flows of water.

WORKING WITH NATURAL FLOWS

In the aftermath of our apparent love affair with concrete and other purely 'hard landscape' approaches to urban planning, there is a renewed interest and emphasis on water-sensitive and other forms of 'green' urban design. A range of novel approaches recognising the value of water flows and other aspects of ecosystems and their processes in the built environment is evolving around the world.

Examples include 'Green Infrastructure,'[15,16] sustainable drainage systems[17] (SuDS, also known as 'source control' in the United States), Community Forests,[18] as well as

---

[14] Wittfogel, K.A. (1957). *Oriental Despotism: A Comparative Study of Total Power.* Yale University Press.

[15] http://www.greeninfrastructure.co.uk/improve.html, accessed 26 May 2020.

[16] Tzoulas K., *et al.* (2007). Promoting ecosystem and human health in urban areas using green infrastructure: A literature review. *Landscape and Urban Planning*, 81(3), pp. 167–178.

[17] Woods, B., *et al.* (2007). *The SUDS Manual.* CIRIA Report C697, Construction Industry Research and Information Association, London.

[18] http://www.communityforest.org.uk/aboutenglandsforests.htm, accessed 26 May 2020.

techniques such as green roofs[19] and rain gardens.[20] In Australia and other nations such as Singapore, the term water-sensitive urban design (WSUD) is widely used as a land planning and engineering design approach that integrates the management of storm water, groundwater, wastewater and water supply into urban design to minimise environmental degradation and improve aesthetic and recreational appeal.[21] For example, the Sydney Metropolitan Catchment Management Authority's (CMA) Water Sensitive Urban Design (WSUD) Program[22] is assisting the transition towards a vision of a 'Water Sensitive City'.

All of these 'green' technologies exploit or emulate natural processes to retain or restore a range of benefits provided by water systems and other ecosystems including natural control of flood regulation, groundwater recharge, pollution abatement, provision of 'green spaces', carbon sequestration and breaking down urban 'heat islands'. This then goes way beyond some altruistic aspiration to bring a bit of greenery and open water into cities. For example, the New York City 'Green Infrastructure Plan' records that the integration of green infrastructure into a mix of more traditional urban infrastructure saves the city approximately $1.5 billion annually over a 'grey only' (reliance on heavy traditional engineering) approach.[23] Incorporating the value of water and other ecosystems into urban planning can also directly increase the value of real estate relative to denser development, with proximity to water and green spaces elevating house values by around 8%[24] as well as providing benefits such as better management of flood risk.[25]

WATER WORLDS

As I reflect in Chapter 16, *No Place Like Home*, water in the environment characterises the places we live and often features in the names of our settlements as bridges, mouths, fords, hams, mills, meres, pools, more directly by reference to a river or coastal name, and indeed in many other ways. Water systems and humanity are indivisible, physically and emotionally, part of which is reflected in the ways we bring water features into our townscapes, shopping malls, business parks, waiting rooms and other developments.

Water features across the world — the Alhambra Palace in Spain, outside the Forbidden City in central Beijing, imposing fountains in London's Trafalgar Square and in other great cities and so on and on — speak of might and wealth. Other water

---

[19] Gill, S.E., Handley, J.F., Ennos, A.R. and Pauleit, S. (2008). Adapting cities for climate change: the role of the green infrastructure. *Built Environment*, 33(1), pp. 122–123.

[20] Grant, G. (2012). *Ecosystem Services Come to Town: Greening Cities by Working with Nature*, John Wiley & Sons: Chichester.

[21] http://www.wsud.org/, accessed 26 May 2020.

[22] http://www.sydney.cma.nsw.gov.au/our-projects/water-sensitive-urban-design-in-sydney-program-water-wsud.html, accessed 26 May 2020.

[23] C40 Cities. (2012). *The NYC Green Infrastructure Plan*. C40 Cities. (https://www.c40.org/case_studies/the-nyc-green-infrastructure-plan, accessed 2020.)

[24] CABE. (2005). *Does Money Grow in Trees?* Commission for Architecture and the Built Environment: London.

[25] Petts, G., Heathcote, J and Martin, D. (2001). *Urban Rivers: Our Inheritance and Future*, IWA Publishing: London.

sources and watercourses, from the smallest holy spring in Ireland to the mighty River Ganges sacred to well in excess of a billion Hindus not merely in India but as a global diaspora, carry spiritual and cultural meanings. Rivers and the greater water cycle carry not merely chemicals, energy and life, but also a host of meanings, history and aspirations for the future.

As I lie in my bath, I am immersed in and enjoying the cleansing and relaxing properties of the river, its flows of matter born in the gas clouds that condensed to form our small blue planet and its journey throughout ecological and human history. I am thereby connected with all of nature, living and non-living elements alike, via this bath full of the planet's water, warmed and briefly detained by human technology in its transit through the grand planetary water cycle that is such a vital vector for nutrients, carbon, energy and other matter, including the dirt from my body.

I may be enjoying the quiet space of the bath as sanctuary from life's pressures, but life itself is nevertheless vital and all around me in the water, as it is in every moment that I breathe the planet's air and eventually lie decomposing in its soil.

7 A Breath of Fresh Air

We may perceive ourselves as terrestrial beasts or perhaps, as suggested in Chapter *Bath Time*, 'water babies'. Yet, in reality, we are as much denizens of an ocean of gases and energy that surrounds us each and every second of our waking and sleeping lives. For all our indivisibility from it, the air is a medium about which we remain barely conscious. As Plato, the Greek philosopher, put it some 2000 years ago: '...*for we are dwelling in a hollow of the earth, and fancy that we are on the surface; and the air we call the heaven, and in this we imagine the stars move. But this is also owing to our feebleness and sluggishness, which prevent our reaching the surface of the air: for if any man could arrive at the exterior limit, or take the wings of a bird and fly upward, like a fish who puts his head out and sees this world, he would see a world beyond; and, if the nature of man could sustain the sight, he would acknowledge that this was the place of the true heaven and the true light and the true stars*'.[1]

EMBEDDED IN THE AIR SPACE

Take a breath and hold it. Exhale slowly. Breathe in again and feel the air rush into your lungs, but this time try to hold it for as long as you can. Register how your body, slowly at first yet with progressively more urgency, compels you to exhale and to gasp for another breath. Evolution has hard-wired us to keep breathing, placing control of our indivisible connection with the air space beyond conscious meddling.

We can see this in the way evolution has shaped our brains to place the most fundamental control of breathing beyond conscious intervention. All vertebrate brains share a common underlying form based on three swellings at the front of the neural

---

[1] From the translation by Benjamin Jowett (2012). *Trial and Death of Socrates*. Barnes & Noble Library of Essential Reading.

tube, which develop into the forebrain, midbrain and hindbrain, respectively. In fishes and amphibians, the three portions remain about the same size, yet the forebrain expands substantially in higher vertebrates including the massive expansion of the cerebral cortex in higher mammals and particularly humans. However, it is the primitive brainstem, the posterior third of the brain also often referred to as the 'reptile brain' reflecting its evolutionary heritage long before the arrival of consciousness. It is the hind brain that retains subconscious control of vital bodily processes including cardiac and respiratory function, consciousness, eating, sleep cycles and breathing. This control centre is fed by a host of sensors to inform it of changing blood chemistry and chest expansion, and it is the hindbrain that tailors breathing to bodily needs and state of arousal. Whether sleeping, wakeful, distracted, running or unconscious, control of our breathing lies beyond conscious tinkering.

Between three and four litres of air surges down our tracheae (windpipe) each time we inhale, dividing down two bronchi which bifurcate repeatedly to feed approximately 300 million fine grapelike sacs, known as alveoli, with a collective internal surface of moist blood-rich tissue more or less the same area as a tennis court. Here, oxygen passes into the bloodstream where it binds with around 25 billion red blood cells that transport it throughout the body. Spent carbon dioxide is released into the air once again by the reverse route.

Assuming an average of between 12 and 17 breaths per minute at rest, and as much as 80 when we exert ourselves, we breathe the air in and out at the very least 20,000 times, and probably in excess of 30,000, each and every day. By the age of 20, we will have taken well in excess of 100 million breaths. So, the simple act of taking a breath of fresh air is in fact quite a thing of wonder!

THE ATMOSPHERE AND US

The connections that we make with every breath are more profound even than this. The planetary atmosphere is, by orders of magnitude, the largest habitat on our home planet yet also one that we most profoundly overlook.[2] Virtually all of the matter forming the air today was present in the dust cloud from which the early planet formed, though its composition has changed dramatically as the planet evolved.

As heavier matter condensed into a planetary core, the primordial planetary atmosphere is thought to have comprised as much as 98% carbon dioxide. Through the 'greenhouse effect', in which heat is trapped by gases such as carbon dioxide (as we discussed in Chapter 6, *Bath Time*), this resulted in an atmospheric temperature of between 85 and 110°C. However, as the Earth cooled, water formed and, with it, the weathering of rock and the start of soil formation, ultimately promoting and in turn accelerated by the genesis of life.

Living things have subsequently profoundly shaped the atmosphere. Perhaps the most profound transition in the 3.85 billion year tenure of life on this world occurred some 2.5–2.7 billion years ago with the evolution of photosynthesis,

---

[2] Everard, M. (2015). *Breathing Space: The Natural and Unnatural History of the Air*. Zed Books: London.

ultimately resulting in the oxygen-rich atmosphere we inhabit today. The very existence of as high a proportion as 21% of such a reactive gas as oxygen in the modern lower atmosphere is an indication of the workings of life. This fact that life creates such dramatic instability in the chemistry of the atmosphere was not lost on British scientist James Lovelock when he was working on NASA-sponsored research into the most effective means for detecting life on other planets. Indeed, this awareness was the basis for the Gaia hypothesis (also discussed in the Chapter 6, *Bath Time*) that conceptualises the Earth's biosphere of closely co-evolved ecosystems and species, each contributing to and benefiting from the stability of the whole, as a homeostatic (self-maintaining) super-organism.

We humans too play our part, consuming oxygen but also contributing to the supply of carbon dioxide that plants in turn use to generate the complex chemicals that we eat whilst at the same time regenerating the oxygen. Some of this free oxygen is converted by interaction with incoming high-energy radiation from space into ozone in the upper atmosphere, forming an 'ozone layer' in the stratosphere that shields the Earth's surface from ultraviolet and other damaging ionising radiation from the sun and the wider universe. This created conditions enabling life to evolve in the now-protected shallow waters and terrestrial surfaces of this world, where it still persists and proliferates today. The stratosphere too burns up meteors before they can inflict harm on the land surface. So, the modern atmosphere that we inhale with each breathe is a product of the collective action of all the living things with which we share this Earth, and have shared it throughout evolutionary time scales.

INTEGRATION WITH ALL OF LIFE

This intimate connection with the airspace via our lungs, bloodstream and brain processing connects us with all of the rest of life, from the photosynthetic activities of plants that regenerate the oxygen that sustains our metabolism through to the moisture, smells, dust, spores and other biological matter that suffuses the air. The air too is the vector of the weather systems that shape the landscape, water the soil, and cycle chemicals and energy.

Through vibrations in the air, we hear the noises of the movement of water and air and other clues to help us navigate the environments we inhabit. We send and receive sounds, connecting with other life forms of our own and other species. Air transmits the light that we detect as sight. It also conveys the chemicals that we detect as smell and, in other species, the pheromones released as hormones external to the body that serve to communicate with other members generally of their own species.

The air space supports even more aspects of our life and livelihood needs. From it, we mine nitrogen to manufacture fertilisers, we disperse waste gases from our domestic fires, industrial processes and internal combustion engines, and we also suspend aeroplanes and fragrances in it. We use it to spread messages of love and inspiration, but also to carry chemical weapons.

We have massively changed the wetlands, forests, soils and the other productive systems with which we evolved, and which are part of the complex and interconnected systems that sustain the homeostatic biospheric system. By so doing, we are progressively unravelling the atmosphere's stability and so many of the gifts we derive from it, yet largely take for granted. Also, because we have for too long omitted to value them, our activities cause our host air space unintended harm ranging from damage to the ozone layer, amplifying the greenhouse effect and accumulating all manner of pollutants.

Because we are so intimately interdependent with it, the harm we cause to the air and atmosphere inevitably causes us harm in return. We live in challenging times as we seek different ways to live, better to recognise and protect the future of the air space that sustains us through every breath we take.

So, with every breath, we connect with all of life. We connect with life in the past through its role in creating and stabilising the atmosphere, in the present with all that shares our home planet, and in the future with all living things that will exchange the substances we exhale.

All this in the simple, everyday act of drawing a breath of fresh air.

8 The Wood for the Trees

Whether an urban street tree, part of a hedge or a forest, a standard specimen or else elements of our gardens, trees are all around us. Do we stop and think often enough about what they do, and how they serve us?

The European landscape was vastly more wooded before the mass felling of its once-extensive forests, attributed initially to our Iron Age forebears then accelerated massively by Roman occupation clearing land for grazing of introduced sheep. Wildwoods covered hills, plains and valleys. They shaped the ever-changing courses of rivers, breaking them into braided networks as channels became choked by fallen wood, another formerly ubiquitous feature of riverscapes also significantly influenced by the activities of once-widespread beavers, the push of diverted river water sweeping clear new channels and moist floodplains which in turn over longer time-scales reverted back to climax wooded cover. This dynamic mosaic supported a diversity of wildlife, from the aurochs — progenitors of modern cattle — that grazed spaces scoured clear by spates and which became quickly vegetated by a profusion of grasses and low flowering plants, through to forest-dwelling creatures of all types.

So, the treescapes of our most 'natural' modern places are far from that. Yet, trees remain a common feature of the world's landscapes regardless of our reckless history of clearances.

LESSONS FROM A FALLEN BIRCH TREE

I broke with tradition during the Easter of 2014. Normally, my tradition was to keep working away at my computer, punctuated by sporadic chocolate egg-related respites with my then younger family. But, that particular Easter, I did what most people seem to do and worked around the garden instead. Specifically, we spent a day or so completing the felling and clearing up of a silver birch (*Betula pendula*) tree that had grown to about 40 feet tall and was posing a potential threat to our and neighbouring properties, given the increasing incidences of high winds. As you may well know, larger silver birch trees are wont to tip over suddenly in storms, their shallow root plates ripping from the soil and all that weight crashing down catastrophically onto whatever lies beneath... in this case, expensive property in several directions!

I do not like cutting down trees, particularly not those that are around 40 years old. So, it was timely to reflect on how this birch tree had been serving us during its long and patient life.

Well, there is the visual beauty of the papery bark and the fine leaves and pendant twigs of the silver birch. This is evident both on a specimen tree but also in other locations as part of a mixed forest, including as a mature tree that may stand out from surrounding saplings. The tree's roots draw nutrients from deep in the soil, re-circulating them on the soil surface as leaves fall to fertilise the understory contributing to the cycles that sustain all the connected organisms of the forest ecosystem. The twigs and leaves provide dappled shade suiting woodland tree and flowering plant species, particularly springtime bulbs such as bluebells (*Hyacinthoides non-scripta*) and rhizomes of plants like the wood anemone (*Anemone nemorosa*) that prosper in a short above-ground life cycle before the canopy grows too dense. They also create a microclimate of stilled air that retains moisture in cycles of evaporation and interception. Water becomes trapped from moisture in the passing air column by the fili-gree of twigs, entering the open structure of the soil beneath the tree's canopy. And the tonnage of carbon locked into roots, twigs, forest litter and wood — carbon we used from our tree 18 months or so later when the logs had dried enough for our log burner reducing demands on our air source heat pump-based heating system — clearly has a role to play in bigger climatic cycles.

Silver birch leaves serve as a food source for literally hundreds of species of insect, the dead wood constituting habitat and food for countless more. Woodpecker species and long-tailed tits (*Aegithalos caudatus*) feed from the insect larder, whilst siskins (*Carduelis spinus*) and other birds feast on birch seeds. Various birds find nesting places in the boughs and in holes in the trunk. Several species of fungi, including the iconic yet toxic and hallucinogenic red-with-white-spotted fly agaric (*Amanita muscaria*) in Europe, a staple of both folklore and fairy tales, are uniquely or particularly associated with silver birches. Our one tall silver birch tree also served as a stepping stone across the fringe of the village in which we live for wildlife such as squirrels, long-tailed tits and the great spotted woodpecker (*Dendrocopos major*).

Beyond their ecological importance, birch trees also symbolised renewal and purification in early Celtic mythology. Bundles of birch twigs are still used in places to drive out the spirits of the old year, whilst traditional besoms (brooms made of bundles of birch twigs) serve both as practical implements and in a more ritual sense to 'purify' gardens. The birch — sometimes known as the 'giving tree' — is also symbolic of love and fertility in folklore, both in human contexts but also reportedly in stock management for which it is used to enhance the fertility of cows.

Because silver birch timber is tough and heavy, it is suitable for furniture-making as well as for handles and toys. Traditionally, birch wood was also turned to manufacture the hard-wearing bobbins, spools and reels used in Lancashire's once-widespread cotton mills. And the bark too has uses including for the tanning of leather and (for American birch species) for traditional Indian birch bark canoes. Salycilate chemicals derived from birch bark have been used effectively against warts. Other herbal properties attributed to birch leaves, twigs and other parts include their laxative, diuretic, anti-rheumatic, stimulant, astringent, anti-helminthic, choloagogue (promoting the flow of bile) and diaphoretic (stimulation of sweating) qualities.

The absence of just this single silver birch tree from our garden became immediately striking in many ways, including how much evening light played on the garden and the back of the house, potentially reducing our need for electric lighting so early in the evening. This was just one element of a significant change in microclimate, part of which included notably greater breeziness that, amongst other effects, dries the washing quicker. This same effect on microclimate would also influence the evaporation of water from other parts of the garden ecosystem. Our silver birch tree was dropped to avert the potential for damage from it falling in a storm, but clearly it also had a powerful role in absorbing wind energy and consequently protecting the vicinity from storm damage.

So, from the practical to the natural, the spiritual to the cultural, the everyday silver birch tree carries with it a host of meanings and utilities, multiple economic and non-economic values and a key role in maintaining nature's essential supportive cycles.

We missed that silver birch tree. However, we planted other native trees to replace it, in particular hazel (*Corylus avellana*) and crab apple (*Malus sylvestris*) that are smaller and so more in scale with the garden. The natural processes of the lost garden tree live on, albeit in different forms.

CRACK WILLOW

Another common tree that we can see from the house is the crack willow (*Salix fragilis*), many of them in fact lining the river as it winds along the fields behind. In the river valley below the scarp upon which our house sits, the river and ditch lines are marked by tall crack willows, one of Britain's largest native willow species. The crack willow can grow up to 25 metres (82 feet) tall and is widely distributed across Europe and Western Asia, particularly beside watercourses and pools. The characteristically deeply fissured bark of an older willow, as well as its fine twigs and slender, oval leaves, are familiar sights in both rural and urban areas.

The name 'crack willow' derives from the tendency of the wood to split, fallen trunks and dislodged twigs and branches readily rooting to produce new willow trees often carried by water some distance from where they fall. These willow saplings and the mighty trees that grow from them play a major role in stabilising riverbanks, offering perch from which kingfishers (*Alcedo atthis*) launch themselves to prey on fish, and their submerged roots offer spawning, nursery, feeding, refuge and ambush habitat for fish.

But willows are of far wider value to nature and people beyond being characteristic and charismatic elements of the landscapes we enjoy. They too absorb much of the storm energy that sweeps the landscape, sheltering stock and averting damage to crops and property. There is also a mutually beneficial relationship between bees and some other insects, food exchanged for fertilisation of willow flowers. Various willow species also feed a wide diversity of other insects including the caterpillars of the puss moth, eyed hawk-moth and red underwing moth, and their branches make good nesting and roosting sites for birds.

All species of willow trees also have cultural significance going right back through recorded history. They are referred to in poetry, in Shakespeare's *Hamlet*, and in ceremonial occasions, having been used as substitutes for palm branches to celebrate Palm Sunday in northern regions. The slender stems of willow shoots are used for basket-weaving, for the manufacture of fish traps and wattle fences. The wattle in 'wattle and daub' house walls was often woven from willow shoots, also used for traditional Welsh boats known as coracles, and wicker ware has a long history with many applications. The wood of the willow has also been used to manufacture brooms, boxes, furniture, toys and musical instruments and a host of other products, with extracts of willow used for tanning, as fibre, and as a constituent of paper, rope and string, and for the manufacture of charcoal. The cricket bat willow, a hybrid of white willow and crack willow, is used, as the name suggests, for the manufacture of cricket bats. Today, willow is now often grown as a biofuel owing to its fast growth rate, particularly on waterlogged and therefore marginal agricultural land. Willows also serve as effective media in constructed wetlands for wastewater treatment and remediation of contaminated land.

There are many more direct uses of various species of willows, to which may be added the various uses of willow products in traditional medicines. The leaves and bark of the willow tree are referred to in ancient texts from Assyria, Sumer and Egypt as a remedy for rheumatic aches and fever.[1] Hippocrates, the Ancient Greek physician, wrote about the diverse medicinal properties of willows in the 5th century BC, whilst willows have also been a staple medicinal treatment of Native Americans across the Americas. Furthermore, the chemical salicin, derived from willows and taking its name from their Latin genus name *Salix*, is metabolised in the human body into salicylic acid which is the precursor of aspirin, the first 'wonder drug' of the modern era which came into production in 1897[2] giving rise subsequently to a hugely important class of drugs known as nonsteroidal anti-inflammatory drugs (NSAIDs).

---

[1] Breasted, James. (Undated English translation). The Edwin Smith Surgical Papyrus. (http://www.touregypt.net/edwinsmithsurgical.htm, accessed 24 July 2014).

[2] *An Aspirin a Day Keeps the Doctor at Bay*. (http://www.nobelprizes.com/nobel/medicine/aspirin.html, accessed 26 May 2020.)

From their diverse significant roles in ecosystems to their broad ceremonial, utilitarian, medicinal and structural uses, not to mention their contribution to landscapes valued by people, there is nothing 'everyday' about a willow tree. Without them, our lives would be immensely poorer, not to mention more vulnerable.

YEW

The European yew (*Taxus baccata*), more commonly referred to simply as the yew, is another common tree found in the cities, towns and the countryside of Britain, though it has a wider distribution right across Europe, into north west Africa and northern Iran, and also south west Asia. In common with other 'everyday' trees, yews play important roles in both natural systems and human and community wellbeing.

One of the more amazing facts about yew trees is their longevity. They can live as long as 400–600 years, and sometimes very much longer with some claimed (albeit contested) ages of up to 5,000–9,500 years.[3] Partly, this great longevity is enabled by the ability of yew trees to split and regenerate without succumbing to disease as readily as other trees, which means that there is often no very ancient timber left from which to make a confident dating of when the tree first germinated. But, whatever their exact longevity, yew trees are the longest-lived of all plants in Europe by some margin, with some living trees, for example, taking root initially in the Mediaeval Age or potentially even before the Christian era.

It is this great longevity that results in characteristic specimen trees central to, and often giving special meaning to, communities right across the natural range of the species. For example, the Fortingall yew in Perthshire, Scotland, has the largest recorded trunk girth in Britain, and is estimated to have grown there for between 2,000 and 3,000 years. In Spain, *Teixu l'Iglesia* stands 15 metres (49 feet) tall with a trunk diameter of 6.82 metres (22.4 feet) and was declared a Natural Monument in 1995 by the Asturian government.[4] This great longevity is also one of the qualities explaining the breadth of spiritual and cultural values ascribed to the yew tree. Yews, for example, are often found in churchyards across the UK and northern Europe, though their common occurrence at these locations is suggested also to have resulted from the tendency of church builders to take over existing pre-Christian sacred sites at which yews may already have been present for their symbolic importance. Certainly, in some traditions and no doubt tied to their great longevity and resilience, the yew is a symbol of transcendence over death. The yew is also ascribed as a link between land and people, including connections with ancestors and ancient religions.

[3] Lewington, A. and Parker, E. (1999). *Ancient Trees: Trees That Live for a Thousand Years.* Collins & Brown Ltd.: London.

[4] Gobierno del Principado de Asturias. (Undated). *Red Ambiental de Asturias: Monumentos Naturales.* Gobierno del Principado de Asturias. (https://www.asturias.es/portal/site/medioambiente/menuitem. 1340904a2df84e62fe47421ca6108a0c/?vgnextoid=fe216c79ae973210VgnVCM10000097030a0aRCRD& vgnextchannel=33d53d6b6311b110VgnVCM1000006a01a8c0RCRD&i18n.http.lang=es, accessed 26 May 2020.)

Most parts of the yew tree are highly toxic, the leaves remaining so even when dried. This is of course part of an adaptation to prevent excessive grazing, exemplifying the many evolutionary adaptations of species to the ecosystems of which they are a part (which we also observed in Chapter 2, *Reading the Tea Leaves* and Chapter 5, *A Simple Bowl of Rice*). But this highly evolved example of 'chemical warfare' also has major benefits for human wellbeing in terms of the diversity of medicinal uses of yew. Significant amongst this pharmacopeia is the molecule taxol — better known by its pharmacological name of Tamoxifen — which has powerful and now widely used anti-cancer properties that enhance the lives of many people around the world significantly including survivors of breast cancer.

Other human uses of the yew have included the manufacture of spear heads[5] made from the easily worked wood that is the hardest of the so-called softwoods. Famously, yew has been used in the making of longbows, exploiting both the durability and springiness of the timber. Yew is also a favoured timber for the building of lutes, and as a preferable timber for woodworking that formerly saw royal monopolies across Europe on the trade and growth of yew. Yews are also widely used in horticulture, including for topiary and also for bonsai, and as a dense wind break maintaining microhabitats in gardens, cityscapes and landscapes. Also, as a poison.

RECOGNISING THE VALUE OF TREES

Just look out of the window now, whether you are in an urban or a rural setting. Count and name the trees, and wonder at their total cumulative beneficence to society. They provide shade and cooling, a bulkhead against the destructive power of storms, a store of carbon and vehicles for the recycling of water and nutrients. They play host to a wealth of wildlife, from insects that brighten our days and prey upon potential pests on our crops and garden plants, and they feed and house birds and a variety of other creatures. They have cultural meaning and offer spiritual enrichment, and they grow with mythologies as dense as the rings marking the accretion of their long-lived trunks. They also serve us with a storehouse of medicines in wide use and yet to be realised. Whether an urban street tree or countryside hedge or forest, trees are doing this 24/7. Their loss would be as catastrophic as their value is underappreciated.

And all this is without considering the many vital things that forests do in stabilising the global climate through their capture and storage of vast reserves of carbon, as well as the ways in which they profoundly change local climate. For example, wooded valleys in arid landscapes can appear green and lush due to the efficient recapture and recirculation of evaporated moisture, retaining water in tight cycles in the landscape and sustaining valuable water resources as well as a diversity of wildlife. At a grander scale, as much as 90% of the rainfall of the extensive rainforest of the Congo Basin is generated by the forest itself, and the

---

[5] White, T.S., Boreham, S., Bridgland, D.R., Gdaniec, K. and White, M.J. (2008). *The Lower and Middle Palaeolithic of Cambridgeshire*. English Heritage Project.

massive rainforests of Amazonia have huge significance for water flows and climate systems globally. The rainforest and dry forest habitat of India's thin band of Western Ghats mountains adjacent to the Arabian Sea are also of vast importance for the whole Deccan Peninsula, intercepting moisture from humid air blowing in from the Arabian Sea and retaining it to sustain the flows of the three great rivers — the Cauvery, Krishna and Godavari — without which so much of the peninsula would be arid and unable to sustain the livelihoods of hundreds of millions of people.

Elsewhere, nature has evolved trees, as well as beetles and herbs, efficient in the capture of moisture from thin air. One such is the Norfolk Island pine (*Araucaria heterophylla*) that has evolved to capture moist air on Norfolk Island off eastern Australia, though this tree is now a common standard tree planted around the world. Evaporation from forest systems globally also contributes massively to 'atmospheric rivers', comprising plumes of concentrated moisture in the atmosphere that may be several thousand kilometres long yet only a few hundred kilometres wide, playing particularly significant roles in the global transport of water vapour[6] as described in Chapter 6, *Bath Time*.

MAKING SPACE FOR TREES

Yet we, an allegedly ecologically enlightened family, cut down our silver birch tree. We did so for the legitimate reason of averting the potential for property damage. But the legitimisation of tree felling nevertheless has consequences for all of these natural services and more. And each loss represents yet another cut to the gross integrity and resilience of the natural world, and its capacities to protect and support us into the future. We have, of course, replanted with native trees of smaller species to offset some of the loss of natural services. However, this everyday gardening tale highlights the conflict of excessive human population with ecosystem extent and quality.

With approaching 7.8 billion people on this planet at the time of writing, getting on for 67 million of us in the UK, we have to think in a far more connected way about how much space we allow for nature in town planning, rural land uses and our everyday exploitation of and interactions with nature. And we have to think fast and strategically as human numbers boom, with the probability of some 9.5–10.5 of us exploitative bipeds occupying the Earth by 2050. Without foresight, the incremental effects of each act of property protection, forest clearance for timber exploitation or food production, and other measures to address legitimate needs will eliminate more of nature's services as we sprawl out more widely across the Earth's habitable surface.

It is these essential yet underappreciated services to humanity from nature, exemplified in this case by the natural services of our felled tree and the other common trees in the places we inhabit, that we have regarded as inconsequential at

---

[6] Zhu, Y. and Newell, R.E. (1994). Atmospheric rivers and bombs. *Geophysics Research Letters*, 21(18), pp. 1999–2002.

least throughout industrial history but probably since the great Iron Age forest clearances.

But we can afford to disregard them no more. We have instead to learn to co-exist, and to think and act more sympathetically with the multiple functions of the landscapes and waterscapes we inhabit, and in the ways we grow food and develop housing, industry and infrastructure. Otherwise, we may find that our everyday cumulative 'legitimate needs' overwhelm the capacity of birch, willow, yew and other trees and the rest of nature to support and secure a decent future for ourselves and those yet to come.

And who would have suspected that this rich tapestry of benefits was weaved from something as everyday as a tree?

9 Unappealing Creatures

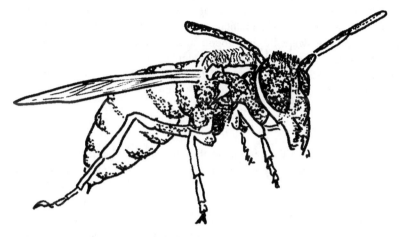

From the metallic cobalt brilliance of the morpho butterfly (*Morpho didius* and a few related species) to the feral beauty of a big cat, the elegance of the natural world is stunning in both form and function. Judged purely on the time devoted to these types of creatures in television footage, you could be forgiven for believing that nature is all, or at least by majority, 'bright and beautiful'. A similar conclusion could be drawn from exploration of the majority of nature conservation efforts that have, by majority, focused on charismatic species.

And yet nature is and does more, so much more, through networks of organisms finely tuned and integrated throughout the expanse of evolution to work together creating a seamless, sustainable whole. It is to the commonplace, the frequently ugly and creepy, and the microscopic and as yet unknown that we owe our greatest thanks. Indeed, the vast bulk of the creatures with which we share this world are poorly known and understood, with many wholly unknown to science or known only to a few specialists. A whole lot more of nature is completely invisible to us. Some organisms might generally be perceived as downright unpleasant! Yet, all play important roles as recyclers, grave-robbers, grim reapers, links in food webs, pollinators of plants, transmitters of parasites, soil-turners and many more.

Visual appeal alone can distract us from what may be, in reality, of far greater importance to the supportive functions and resilience of the global ecosystem that plays host to us. For all living things, whether we recognise them or whether we like them or not, are the companions with which we co-evolved. All therefore have a place and roles to play in the complex workings of the planetary ecosystem.

I was stimulated to write this chapter by people asking me questions, generally in my various broadcasts or public meetings when I have been talking about the workings of ecosystems and other facets of nature, about '*What was the point of...*' certain unappealing creatures. OK, some we have an aversion to for reasons that may have good evolutionary roots: snakes, scorpions, possibly some spiders, and

51

their like, though all serve valuable natural functions of which we are ultimate beneficiaries. One mountain campsite I regularly visited in South Africa when working there as a government advisor even had a harmonious relationship with a spitting cobra (one of several species of cobras that can squirt venom from their fangs when defending themselves) that lived behind the pots and pans in the kitchen, the snake keeping the kitchen area rodent-free and not bothering the cooks! Yet, many quite widespread and abundant creatures that are not inherently life-threatening also commonly invoke a shudder for many people.

So, let us now turn our attentions to some of the British and indeed wider public's 'least wanted'.

WHAT'S THE POINT OF SLUGS?

My starting point for this mission is the slug, and in particular addressing the question above which was posed to me over a lunch break by a participant at a public engagement workshop I was running in Birmingham in the English midlands: *'What's the point of slugs?'* Now, I will agree that slugs are not greatly beloved by many amongst the British public. Indeed, they are perceived as, and in fact are, slimy beasts, and they are also wont to munch away at tender garden plants and crops. However, as creatures that have co-evolved with us and which now share our world, they clearly have a role, or roles, to play within nature. Through this, they offer services to humanity that may be as important as they are overlooked.

Many of these slug-based services lie in their various roles in maintaining the functioning and resilience of the ecosystems of which they are inextricable parts, and hence the sustainability of these ecosystems and their capacities to provide benefits to humanity and other species.

Though the aversion of slugs to salt — apart from sea slugs obviously — is well known, let's start with a marine mollusc to explore some of the contributions of the common or garden slugs that we encounter in our terrestrial neighbourhoods. A limpet is a marine rocky shore mollusc with a shell, but is otherwise similar to a slug. When limpets get removed from a rocky shore either by pollution or in scientific experiments, the soft algae on which they feed blooms on the rocks. This, in turn, swamps out much other plant matter, and also spaces for the many characteristic and other animals that naturally occur on rocky shores. This natural weeding function, simultaneously maintaining spaces for more diverse wildlife and converting plant productivity into forms consumed by the predators of molluscs, is exactly the same as the roles that slugs play in the terrestrial environment. Slugs then have an important role to play in nature's weed management, maintaining the diversity of ecosystems and hence their capacities to process substances efficiently and adaptively in changing conditions.

Human—slug conflicts arise as we humans like to grow single species of plants as crops in fields, and as exotic specimens in weed-free gardens. However, as it is simply in the nature of an organism such as a slug to feed on a glut of softer, tastier plants such that overall biodiversity is maintained, people find them little more than annoying pests. Yet, in reality, it is our gloriously manufactured monocultures that perturb the natural diversity and balance of nature.

Through their grazing habits and production of body tissues, slugs make the primary productivity of plants and fungi, including their nutrients and stored solar-derived energy, available to those creatures that eat them. These include, as examples, hedgehogs, badgers, thrushes, frogs, snakes, fish and many more animals besides. Furthermore, overwintering as they do in dead wood, leaf litter and underground, slugs store this goodness between seasons. Slugs thereby play important roles in connecting different levels in food webs, without which the more charismatic members of the global zoo might suffer along with an overall decline in the efficiency and resilience of planetary food and energy cycles.

Slugs, like many molluscs, also play important roles in the transmission of parasitic organisms,[1] often as intermediate hosts, thereby helping nature control balances in, and the wider processes of, ecosystems.

The French are famous for their gastronomic enjoyment of snails — *escargots* — cooked in butter and garlic. A snail is merely a slug in a shell suit, so there is no reason on Earth why slugs should not become nutritious snacks for humanity: a potential service to which we may find ourselves turning increasingly as the burgeoning human population overwhelms nature's capacities to supply other food. In fact, slugs have been eaten by people throughout history. In part, this is due to the medicinal qualities that have been ascribed to them: a former alleged cure for tuberculosis involving swallowing slugs alive.

Though the general populace might find them unappealing, some species of slug are of aesthetic and other cultural values. This includes the endangered Kerry slug (or Kerry spotted slug, *Geomalacus maculosus*) that is found only in restricted regions of Ireland, Spain and Portugal. This large, attractive spotted slug is listed in the Irish Red Data Book[2] as a nature conservation priority, and is protected by law in each country and across Europe under the European Union Habitats Directive.[3] Furthermore, older anglers, particularly those interested in catching chub (*Squalius cephalus*) in rivers, will tell you what good baits slugs are for their quarry. Slugs have also featured in movies such as *Flushed Away*[4] and *Harry Potter and the Chamber of Secrets*.[5] You can also readily buy mugs, tee-shirts and other giftware bearing slug motifs (as yet another example of the seemingly inexhaustible market opportunities presented by an internet search). So, the cultural services that slugs offer to enrich our lives are surprisingly well represented for a creature so vilified by many!

We could go on and on exploring the beneficial services that slugs confer upon humanity. But the brief considerations above already demonstrate some of the breadth of benefits they serve to us. So, even if you do not find yourself in rapture

---

[1] For example: Thomas. F. and Poulin, R. (1998). Manipulation of a mollusc by a trophically transmitted parasite: convergent evolution or phylogenetic inheritance? *Parasitology*, 116, pp. 431–436. Also: Lee, H.G. (1995). Mollusks and Man: A Medical Perspective. *The Junonia, Newsletter of the Sanibel-Captiva Shell Club*, June 1995.

[2] *Irish Red Data Book*. (1988). Stationary Office, Dublin.

[3] Council Directive 92/43/EEC of 21 May 1992 on the Conservation of Natural Habitats and of Wild Fauna and Flora (http://eur-lex.europa.eu/legal-content/EN/TXT/?uri=CELEX:31992L0043, accessed 26 May 2020.)

[4] Aardman Animations and DreamWorks Animation. (2006). *Flushed Away*.

[5] Warner Bros. Pictures. (2002). *Harry Potter and the Chamber of Secrets*.

about slugs, you may at least appreciate a little more of the hard work that these generally unloved slimy creatures do for us!

WHAT'S THE POINT OF WASPS?

Having considered at least some of the answers to the question *'What's the point of slugs?'* I thought it might be interesting to reflect on another of the least favourite cohabitants of an English summer. Hence, we now turn our attention to considering *'What's the point of wasps?'* For, akin to slugs, the general populace is not, by majority, deeply affectionate about these buzzy, stingy, picnic-raiding beasties. So here we go with a few thoughts about the point, or points, of wasps.

Firstly, let's qualify what we mean by 'wasp'. Wasps are in fact a diverse group of insects, spanning well in excess of 100,000 species globally, with more being discovered. (For the anoraks amongst us, like me, they are in the sub-order *Apocrita* in the order *Hymenoptera*, a sub-order that also includes bees and ants.) Many, if not most, wasps are either predatory or parasitic, almost every pest insect species having at least one species of wasp that preys upon it or parasitises it.

The yellow-and-black banded wasps so familiar at British barbeques, when not driven away by the equally traditional rainfall normally associated with the great British Bank Holiday, belong to a subset of wasps in which the ovipositor (egg-laying appendage) is modified into a venomous sting. However, not every species within this group of wasps possesses a sting. The common insects we most commonly refer to simply as 'wasps' belong to the family Vespidae. (The family Vespidae also includes the hornet, an increasingly scarce insect in the British Isles that is most generally perceived as a steroid-enhanced wasp with a bigger sting and a scarily deep buzz!)

Many of these classic wasps are social, forming colonies in which most of the workers are sterile. It is these sterile workers that we mainly encounter in our gardens and picnics, though large female 'queens' can often be seen in the early spring searching out new locations in which to build a nest and lay eggs. The sterile workers that emerge from these early spring nests then fan out across the land, catching mainly insect and other small prey, which they incapacitate with their stings and bring back to the ever-growing nest to feed larvae tended by other workers.

The combined predatory and parasitic activities of wasps, which increase in number over the summer as colonies grow, mean that they have a massive impact on the control of prey insect populations. This is highly significant in maintaining species balance and the cycling of productivity, nutrients and energy in nature's cycles. So, one of the very important ways in which wasps contribute to human wellbeing is in aiding the production of food, fibre, and horticultural and ornamental resources. In fact, wasps, as a group, are critically important in the natural control of their host and prey organisms. Without them, pests would proliferate, and the extent of crop damage and loss, as well as greater reliance on damaging pesticides and other control measures, would multiply substantially. Wasps thereby provide significant values to gardeners, farmers and horticulturalists and all who benefit from their produce. This is an ever-more important consideration given emerging concerns both about global food security and also the need to reduce our dependence on many of the more harmful synthetic substances that we use today.

Some wasps also feed on pollen as adult insects. In so doing, they benefit ecosystems and people through pollination services. This represents another major benefit for maintaining ecosystem integrity and biological diversity in addition to serving farming, horticulture and gardening interests.

In addition to these services, wasps also serve as important links in food chains. This does not just happen when they die and their bodies are re-absorbed into ecosystems. Though many organisms avoid wasps either by direct learning, or because the yellow-and-black banding is a common code in nature for species that should be avoided as they can sting or bite, a surprisingly diverse group of organisms do indeed eat wasps. These wasp predators include various invertebrates, including several species of dragonflies (*Odonata*), robber and hoverflies (*Diptera*), some other wasp species (*Hymenoptera*), beetles (*Coleoptera*) and moths (*Lepidoptera*). Various vertebrates also feed on wasps, including numerous species of birds (the book *Birds of the Western Palearctic*[6] lists 133 species that at least occasionally consume wasps) and also badgers, bats, weasels, rats and mice and, overseas, animals such as wolverines. Some people too eat wasps, typically as larvae; they are reportedly quite tasty.

As older anglers may know, wasp grubs (larvae) are considered a highly effective bait for many coarse fish species. This indicates their value as a food for other species, but also how wasps support our own recreational activities not to mention an associated lucrative industry for whose brave enough to smoke out their nests to extract the living larvae.

And, of course, the 'cottage industry' of wasp nest removal for other purposes is another contribution to local activities and regional economic activity. So too, the market for antihistamine and other treatments for wasp stings, and for products such as nest-destroying chemicals, swatters and wasp deterrents. Wasps of course also recycle wood, softening it with their saliva and creating a *papier mâché* type substance from which their papery nests are built, and these beautiful, aesthetically pleasing structures have inspired some art and architecture. As we saw in Chapter 4, *Yesterday's Papers*, Cai Lun, the ancient Chinese inventor of paper-making, was said to have been inspired by the nests of wasps and bees.

Wasps have also inspired art, including, for example, Ralph Vaughan-Williams incidental music *The Wasps* (1909). 'Wasp' too is a fictional superheroine character in comic books published by Marvel Comics, first appearing in 1963 and gifted with the ability to shrink to a height of several centimetres, grow to giant size, fly by means of insectoid wings and to fire bioelectric energy blasts. These are just some of the art forms attributed to the real or imagined qualities of wasps!

And, of course, we are discussing wasps here — this and other books referring to wasps constituting yet other forms of creative expression — indicating a far wider set of cultural interests and associations with these 'unappealing creatures', quite aside from their more familiar association with summer, stings and barbeques!

This is not the final word on what wasps do for us, but it is a pretty good first step into addressing the question '*What's the point of wasps?*' There are in fact lots of

---

[6] Snow, D.W. and Perrins, C. (Editors). (1997). *The Birds of the Western Palearctic*. Oxford University Press.

'points', quite apart from that pointy sting that perhaps blinds us to the amazing work they do, and from which we benefit in so many ways!

WHAT'S THE POINT OF WOODLICE?

The general public has a common aversion to other creatures besides slugs and wasps. Based on the reactions of friends, the next on the list of beasts and bugs that freak out the lay populace is the humble woodlouse. Now, this is quite odd as they are so small and harmless, and also mainly nocturnal, so perhaps not encountered often other than when disturbing rotting wood or leaf litter or moving things around in a musty shed or wood pile. It is therefore worth looking at what woodlice actually are and what they do before reserving judgement on the point, or points, of them.

Woodlice are crustaceans, a large group of arthropods (animals with exoskeletons and jointed legs) comprising some 67,000 species of crabs, lobsters, shrimps, crayfish, krill and barnacles. Within this large group of creatures, woodlice are isopods (order *Isopoda*, suborder *Oniscidea*) which, as the name applies, have multiple legs of more or less even size (unlike the modified pincers of crabs and lobsters). There are over 5,000 known species of woodlice globally, including 45 native or naturalised species of woodlouse in the British Isles. Some — the pill bugs — can roll up into an almost perfect defensive sphere, though most species can't do this. All are fascinating creatures, female woodlice retaining fertilised eggs in a pouch known as a marsupium on the underside of the body, keeping the eggs in relative safety until they hatch and disperse as small, white offspring. Female woodlice are also capable of reproducing asexually.

But most woodlice species, with some minor exceptions including a small number of dryland species and some others that have returned to water, need to live in moist places as their exoskeletons are porous and rapidly lose water. Consequently, woodlice are usually nocturnal, venturing out and about when evaporation is at its lowest. This tactic also helps them evade some of the many creatures that feed on them. Woodlice feed mainly on dead plant matter.

Woodlice are known by a wide range of local names, including the charming Wiltshire name 'chuckypigs'. But there is just something about them that some people don't like. I remember being a bit squeamish about them when I was young, though I grew out of it, and my daughter gets the creeps from them though I hope that she will also grow to love them! Putting an exact finger on the reasons for this aversion is tricky, one possible explanation being their association with damp and rotting places which may be creepy for other reasons.

But, squeamish though some of us may be about them, woodlice serve many useful purposes in supporting and regulating processes within the ecosystems of which they are a part. These include eating and recycling detritus, which mainly comprises dead plant matter. They also overturn the soil, maintaining its structure and performing a range of linked functions relating to increasing its porosity to air and water and its carbon and nutrient contents. And, of course, woodlice also constitute important links in food webs, as they are eaten by a diversity of animals including many species of birds, amphibians, reptiles and other animals. Woodlice then have some pretty important roles to play as one of nature's more abundant recyclers, keeping the great cycles of productivity, nutrients and energy turning, and enhancing the functions of the much-neglected yet vital resource of soil (that we'll look at more closely in Chapter 11, *Glorious Mud*). The importance of the humble woodlouse is, it seems, greatly overlooked.

Despite all that, we mainly just find them annoying when they freak us out, feed on the tender plants that we cultivate in our gardens, and nibble at ripening strawberries and tender seedlings. We may also be frustrated when they invade our homes in search of moisture and warmth, particularly when there is damp in the house or when we bring in logs from outside stacks during the winter. (My house is full of woodlice at some points during the year as we use a wood burner in preference to a fossil fuel system for heating!) However, in their favour, and despite their association with rotten places, woodlice do not spread disease nor damage wood other than that which is already rotting, which they help recycle into useful forms available to other organisms.

We are weird in terms of the closely related animals we find repulsive or attractive to eat. Escargots are a delicacy yet slugs are hideous, rabbit is pleasant whilst rats are revolting, and shrimps are a delicacy whilst woodlice are an abomination. Why? Many insects are believed to deliver twice the amount of protein content per unit mass than vertebrate meat, including fish. As human numbers spiral and natural productivity declines, we may have to make more use of edible creatures lower down the food chain. The term used to define the eating of insects, 'entomophagy', is also more widely applied to other invertebrate creatures. The use of creepy crawlies of various kinds — ants, locusts, scorpions and all manner of species we normally shy away from in the West — is practiced surprisingly widely around the world. Over 1,000 species of insects are known to be eaten in 80% of the world's nations,[7] with around 3,000 ethnic groups recorded as practicing entomophagy.[8] However, in some societies, insect-eating is uncommon or even taboo.[9,10] Nevertheless, although insect eating is rare in the developed world, insects remain a popular food in many developing regions of Latin America, Africa, Asia and Oceania. As they are all packed with calcium and protein, it might seem odd to a dispassionate outside observer that we make only highly selective gastronomic use of our wealth of insect, crustacean and other abundant invertebrate fauna. For this and other reasons, some companies are trying to introduce insects into Western diets.[11]

Despite belonging to the same animal group (the crustaceans) as shrimp, crabs, lobsters and crayfish, all of them delicious, raw woodlice are said to have an

---

[7] Carrington, D. (2010). Insects could be the key to meeting food needs of growing global population. *Guardian*, 1 August 2010. (http://www.theguardian.com/environment/2010/aug/01/insects-food-emissions, accessed 26 May 2020.)

[8] Ramos-Elorduy, J. and Menzel, P. (1998). *Creepy Crawly Cuisine: The Gourmet Guide to Edible Insects*. Inner Traditions/Bear & Company. p. 44.

[9] Weiss, M.L. and Mann, A.E. (1985). *Human Biology and Behaviour: An Anthropological Perspective*. Little Brown & Co.: Boston.

[10] Gordon, D.G. (1998). *The Eat-a-Bug Cookbook*. Ten Speed Press: Berkeley, CA.

[11] Thompson, A. (2013). Want to help solve the global food crisis? Eat more crickets. *Forbes*, 7 July 2013. (http://www.forbes.com/sites/ashoka/2013/07/31/want-to-help-solve-the-global-food-crisis-eat-more-crickets/, accessed 26 May 2020.)

unpleasant taste comparable to strong urine. This is hardly likely to get your taste buds going! However, when cooked, this taint goes away. Boiled woodlouse is said to have a shrimp-like flavour, which is not at all surprising given their crustacean lineage. They can be cooked like shrimps, their oceanic cousins. Though the idea may be unappealing given our cultural conditioning, woodlice may just be able to provide a tasty provisioning service in an hour of need if we are starving or if we continue to overwhelm nature's capacity to provide us with nourishment from animal species higher up the food chain!

All in all, woodlice have a diversity of cultural associations. This is in part re-flected in the abundance of local names by which they are known: the already mentioned 'chuckypig' and pill bug, as well as 'roly-poly', 'armadillo bug', 'boat-builder', 'carpenter', 'cheeselog', 'cheesy bug', 'doodlebug', 'potato bug', 'sow bug', 'roll up bug', 'chiggy-peg', 'slater', 'gramersow', 'Grandad', 'butcher boy', 'butchy boy' and 'wood bug'. And that's just the ones that have found their way into Wikipedia[12]!

So, sneer not at the humble woodlouse, for it may just be doing more good for the sustainability of this planet than all of us environmentalists put together!

WHAT'S THE POINT OF PARASITES?

As we have observed, many microbes live out parasitic lives: a relationship in which the parasitic organism lives in or on another organism that derives no clear benefit from the association. So, too, do many other groups of animals and plants. Indeed, of the estimated 6 or so million species of organisms on this planet, 40–50% are parasitic with approximately 75% of links in food webs globally involving a parasitic species.[13] These links in food webs are vital for regulation of the abun-dance of host organisms, potentially for reducing the impact of toxic pollutants and for a wide range of other ecological processes and functions, many of which remain poorly known or completely unknown. Consequently, the beneficial role of para-sitism on such a grand scale has largely been overlooked in research; equally, the costs of extinction of parasites may be significant for the health and abundance of a large number of free-living species and the workings of whole ecosystems.

Despite their ubiquity, their important ecological roles and the benefits they bring, parasites have a bad press. Also, contrary to common perception, not all parasitic organisms are as devastating as, say, the virus responsible for Ebola or the five species of *Plasmodium* microorganisms that cause malaria. Indeed, the more damaging disease-causing parasites may reflect an early stage in their adoption of a new host species as the parasitic organism makes the jump from a long-established host — in the cast of Ebola and malarial diseases into humans.

As parasites must continue to live and reproduce, more highly adapted parasites tend to cause little or no harm to their host organisms. An exception here is those

---

[12] http://en.wikipedia.org/wiki/Woodlouse, accessed 26 May 2020.

[13] Dobson, A. *et al.* (2008). Homage to Linnaeus: How many parasites? How many hosts? *Proceedings of the National Academy of Sciences*, 105(1), pp. 11482–11489.

parasites that rely on one creature eating another to complete their life cycle, as, for example, in the case of flukes (flatworms) of the genus *Diplostomum* that typically infest fish, which they debilitate to ensure that the final host (typically a warm-blooded bird) is better able to catch and digest the fish and its associated load of larval parasites. With this exception, it is otherwise in the interests of long-established parasites to ensure that their hosts continue for as long as possible to feed and transport them, and to distribute their eggs.

This 'minimal harm' rule is certainly the case for human hosts in terms of ta-peworms and many types of small skin mites, not uncommon passengers on and in our bodies about which we may remain blissfully unaware. Also the 'endobiome': the hugely diverse microbial constituents of our guts, skin and other parts of the body. Indeed, emerging research is beginning to tease out the wealth of benefits emerging from a diverse and balanced endobiome for the healthy development of babies and for addressing conditions as diverse as diabetes, irritable bowel syn-drome, dermatitis, diarrhoea and allergic rhinitis.[14] We'll consider the endobiome in more detail in Chapter 17, *99.9% of All Known Germs*.

Both for humans and for all other life forms, it may indeed be the case that our generally negative and ghoulish perception of parasites has blinded us to the many benefits that they may confer, not only to host species but to the workings of entire ecosystems upon which we depend.

ALL THINGS BRIGHT AND BEAUTIFUL?

In nature, aesthetic appeal (by human standards) and function often fit together elegantly. However, this is very far from always holding true. There is, in reality, a deeper form of beauty seen in the elegance with which nature has honed its cast of players to perform functions not only with great efficiency but as part of a concerted whole of intimately integrated cogs. But we cannot get away from the fact that, laying the foundations upon which stands the pantheon of organisms that are charismatic or which we put to work as crops, pets, draught animals or for dec-oration or urban shade, there are legions of ugly, murderous, grimy and slimy or just plain unknown foot soldiers that keep global cycles happening. We neglect this vast bulk of nature at our considerable peril, for we too are nature and without it our lives and our capacity to use and manipulate the world around us to serve our own selfish ends will become inevitably progressively impoverished.

In nature, there is no waste. Without functional connections and purpose, there is only extinction. The natural world is therefore full of grave-robbers, decomposers and munchers of dead and rank matter, without which plant and animal corpses, feces and other wastes would accumulate, and matter and energy would not be recycled and regenerated into new life. Even the parasite must continue to live, and so is adapted to extend its life and, generally, that of its host. It has been fruitful

---

14 Quigley, E.M.M. (2012). Prebiotics and probiotics: Their role in the management of gastrointestinal disorders in adults. *Nutrition in Clinical Practice*, 27(2), pp. 195–200.

reflecting on some of the things that the less appealing members of the global menagerie do, and the ways in which we benefit from their tireless work.

We need to learn to love, or if not love then admire and appreciate, the grim reapers that control the diversity and balance of nature, the grave robbers that tirelessly recycle nutrients and energy, the slugs, wasps, woodlice and myriad other life forms, both known and unknown, and all the other unappealing creatures that are the real heroes in maintaining a vital planetary biosphere and, with it, our own prospects for living a decent quality of life.

We turn to a raft of smaller creatures working tirelessly in keeping the global ecosystem running in Chapter 14, *All Creatures Great But Small*, also later in the book looking at organisms even smaller than that in Chapter 17, *99.9% of All Known Germs*.

10 Fossilised Sunbeams

"The Red Flower?" said Mowgli. "That grows outside their huts in the twilight. I will get some."

This famous line from *The Jungle Book*, the 1894 collection of stories by English author Rudyard Kipling in which most of the characters aside from the 'man cub' Mowgli are wild Indian animals, speaks of fire. The phrase 'Man's red flower' is perhaps more widely known today from the 1967 animated film version of *The Jungle Book* by Walt Disney Productions, in which King Louie — the King of the Apes — sang the song *'I Wanna Be Like You'* (the monkey song) containing the phrase '... *Give me the power of man's red flower, So I can be like you'*.

FOSSILISED SUNLIGHT

So, what, exactly, is this 'red flower'; this strange, near-living thing we call fire that has so fascinated humanity since prehistory?

Aside from meanings relating to discharging a firearm or removing someone from a job, many dictionary definitions of 'fire' tend to converge around the light, heat and often also smoke-emitting process that occurs when substances combine chemically with oxygen. This may be a scientifically sound description, but it is far from all that fire means to humanity.

All of us, I am guessing, will have struck a match, perhaps to light a candle. Many of us, particularly as children, will have been mesmerised by the dance of a flame, be that on the wick of a candle, a gas hob, a bonfire, maybe in a grate in the living room or through the glass of a log burner. There is something mesmerising and far more elusive than just a chemical reaction going on right there in front of our eyes.

In the simple act of lighting a candle — or other flammable material — you are in essence liberating sunlight that fell on the Earth years ago, perhaps even millions of years ago, but that has since been immobilised in fossil form.

Energy embedded in the chemical bonds within oil, gas, coal, timber, wax and other flammable organic matter ultimately derives from the sun. Through the process of photosynthesis, plants capture solar energy to build organic matter from simple inorganic molecules, locking that energy away in chemical bonds. These chemical products and their embedded energy enter food webs, fuelling all living things. Some, such as straw and timber, we might burn directly, particularly in a dried form, liberating embedded energy captured by these plants that same season or else over a number of recent years. Other plants may be grazed by animals, their chemical and energy content transferred along a food chain. Animal dung is a commonplace fuel in many parts of Asia and Africa, rich in partially digested remains of vegetation and enriched by microbes from the guts of livestock. Oils and fats from plants, fish, rendered livestock and other animals distil solar-derived nutrition into energy-rich forms.

Mineral oil, coal and other fossil energy forms derive from anaerobic decomposition of the buried remains of organisms dying anything from several million to 650 million years ago, their solar-fuelled biomass concentrated by compression and geothermal heating into remains with a high energy and carbon content. These residues brew over time into petroleum, coal and natural gas, mined today for uses in chemical manufacturing and as energy sources. The roots of the European Industrial Revolution, a movement that has pervaded the world shaping industrial habits and economic frameworks, is heavily rooted in accessing and releasing the fossilised content of sunlight falling on the planet's surface millions of years ago. We liberate this fossilised energy for contemporary transport, heat and power generation and for waste combustion purposes. Even our cars are solar-powered, be that through releasing fossil solar energy through internal combustion of petrol or diesel, or else by running on electricity generated often by fossil fuel combustion.

In 2018, fossil fuels comprised 85% of the world's primary energy sources, the rest accounted for by nuclear, hydroelectric and other renewable sources. The proportion of renewable energy generation and consumption has since begun to grow sharply as nations have begun to respond to the threats posed by climate change. The year 2019 saw the largest recorded global fall in coal-powered electricity production, not due to direct choices on environmental grounds but resulting from longer-term investment in alternative energy sources reducing their marginal costs.[1] In the first half of 2020, lockdown measures imposed in response to the Covid-19 pandemic accelerated the decline in use of coal, the fuel that powered the Industrial Revolution, for energy generation, renewable energy sources maintaining their strong growth.[2] As of 10th June 2020, Britain's electricity grid had not burnt any coal for 60 days, by far the longest period since the dawn of the Industrial Revolution over 200 years previously, with no anticipation of any change in the foreseeable future. Despite active attempts by US President Donald Trump to support the American coal industry, the United States also consumed more energy from renewable sources than from coal for the first time ever in the first half of 2020, whereas almost half of US electricity was derived from coal only a decade before. Even in India, formerly one of the fastest-growing users of coal, demand fell significantly helping the country reduce its carbon dioxide emissions for the first time in 37 years. Lockdowns in the face of a global pandemic of course create unique circumstances, but transition towards renewable sources of energy and progressive abandonment of carbon-intensive fossil fuels has become a decadal underlying trend.

Renewable solar and wind energy sources are, of course, also powered both directly and indirectly by the sun's energy. Solar energy also has a bearing on tidal power, though the bulk of the driving energy for that is gravitational. Solar inputs also drive the global water cycle upon which hydropower depends.

It is all a matter of short and long cycles. Solar generation uses solar energy falling right now and wind generation harvests solar-driven air currents. Wood uses sunlight falling to Earth a few years ago. By contrast, burning fossil fuels releases sunlight captured by long-extinct vegetation from as far ago as the origins of multicellular life. Just turning on an electric kettle will by large majority tap solar energy, be that generated in real time by renewable sources or by releasing sunbeams trapped in wood or locked away over those unimaginably long timescales in fossil fuel deposits.

FOSSIL SUNLIGHT'S 'EVIL TWIN'

The benefits provided to humanity by unlocking all this fossilised sunshine are manifold. However, these short-term benefits have an insidious 'evil twin'. Planet Earth formed from hot gases some 4.5 billion years ago, when all matter was in free circulation. Over geological timescales, natural precipitation and other processes began to 'sort out' some matter, subsequently accelerated by biomineralisation and other biospheric processes occurring after the emergence of life. Substances that were once abundant in the early atmosphere, such as heavy metals, carbon and nutrient elements such as phosphorus, became progressive locked away into the lithosphere (the rocky and largely inert underground parts of the Earth's crust). Over geological timescales, the biosphere — the living part of the Earth comprising atmosphere, hydrosphere and land — has become inestimably 'cleaner' with respect

[1] Rowlatt, J. (2019). Coal: Is this the beginning of the end? *BBC News: Science & Environment*, 25 November 2019. (https://www.bbc.co.uk/news/science-environment-50520962, accessed 9 June 2020.)

[2] Rowlatt, J. (2020). Could the coronavirus crisis finally finish off coal? *BBC News: Science & Environment*, 9 June 2020. (https://www.bbc.co.uk/news/science-environment-52968716, accessed 9 June 2020.)

to these substances as they have been progressively locked away in inert, rocky forms.

Releasing these fossilised chemicals once again from mined sources into natural systems is in essence a process of returning the biosphere into a former, less pure state. We know the hazards of releasing too much heavy metal, phosphorus and low-grade radioactive material into living systems, their potential to accumulate and cause harm resulting from the inability of complex cellular life and biospheric cycles to process substances with which they have not evolved. The same is true of all that carbon that has been locked away into the Earth's crust over evolutionary timescales once it is emitted again into the atmosphere.

The early planetary atmosphere substantially comprised carbon dioxide, with little or no oxygen but small amounts of gases such as ammonia and methane. Carbon dioxide molecules absorb infrared radiation. This is the basis of the 'greenhouse effect', high concentrations of carbon dioxide acting like a greenhouse, trapping heat in the atmosphere and so raising its temperature and increasing the energy in the climate system. Compounded by greater volcanic activity, the greenhouse effect generated by the high carbon dioxide and methane content of the early Earth were initially sufficient to keep the atmosphere so hot that water could not condense into liquid form. Initial progressive cooling of the planet still created conditions for a long time that were way too hot for what modern life forms could survive. Contrast that with our clement modern atmosphere more of less comprising 79% nitrogen, 21% oxygen and small amounts of other gases including 0.9% argon and 0.04% carbon dioxide. It would be unwise to heat up that stable and moderate state, for example, by substantially increasing the 'greenhouse effect'.

But all those 'fossilised sunbeams' were not locked away in isolation. They were locked away in the form of carbon-rich products of photosynthesis, taking with them the large but progressively declining carbon content of the early atmosphere. And the mass remobilisation of that fossilised carbon to liberate its stored energy content is the primary driver of climate change, through increasing global atmospheric carbon dioxide concentrations. The 'evil twin' of the modern world's heavy reliance on fossil fuel-based energy systems is the return to the atmosphere of excess carbon dioxide, effectively returning the atmosphere to a prior evolutionary state, warming the planet and placing us all in peril. Without largely rebalancing the removal of carbon dioxide from the atmosphere with inputs into it, as is the case in natural biospheric cycles maintaining atmospheric chemistry, the carbon content of fossil fuels that had taken millions of years to form can only put us all in grave danger if burned over short-term human timescales. The trends of fossil energy exploitation by the global human population accounted for 567 TeraWatt hours (TWh) in 1850, rising to 5,972, 20,139 and 94,462 TWh, respectively, in 1900, 1950 and 2000, and still rising to 133,853 TWh in 2017 despite various global agreements to curtail dependence on fossil fuels as a key adaptation measure to address run-away global climate change.[3]

---

[3] Ritchie, H. and Roser, M. (2020). Fossil fuels. ourworldindata.org. (https://ourworldindata.org/fossil-fuels, accessed 26 May 2020.)

This is not the place to expand on the challenges of climate change and the other options that we have available to transform societal energy systems, nor our duties to the future of humanity and planetary life to arrest worrying climate change trends. However, the lesson is salutary that, in our use of energy, we are utterly dependent on the processes of ecosystems, whether that energy was captured by ecosystems right now or else millions of years ago. Also, if we are not careful, we create pressures that threaten the balance and viability of the very natural life support system upon which we are utterly reliant.

A NATURALLY REGENERATIVE FORCE

In common with many other of our common misrepresentations of the outcomes of ecosystem processes — such as flood risk incurred by things we build on flood-plains, portrayal of all 'germs' as bad, or fear of overwhelmingly benign and in fact hugely beneficial wild animals — fire also has an undeservedly bad reputation. It is of course distressing to see people's homes and possessions going up in flames, or worse still loss of human and natural life in wild fires. It would be salutary to not build dwellings and infrastructure in fire prone areas in the first place, as indeed avoiding building in floodplains which — the clue is in the name — do actually flood! But fire is both a natural and a regenerative force.

Whilst large wildfires may strike fear into public and political minds, some plants and animals are not only adapted to periodic fires, but are even dependent upon the effects of fire to make the environment more hospitable for their re-generation and growth. 'Fire ecology' is a branch of science addressing the origins of fire in ecosystems and its influence in shaping fire-prone ecosystems. Fire creates an open seed bed, preparing the soil for seeding and enriching it with nutrients both liberated from the soil by heat and through deposition of ash. It also eliminates other competitive plants, as well as removing undergrowth permitting sunlight to reach the forest floor and so enhancing overall plant and wider biological diversity. Fire also tends to kill off older or diseased trees, and with them reserves of insect pests, leaving younger and healthier trees to grow with less competition. Burned trees may also provide habitat for nesting birds, mammals, insects and other wildlife, charred remains also drip-feeding a return of nutrients into the soil. There are also risks following wildfires, of course, as surface layers of leaf litter rich in organic matter and associated small living things are removed, also potentially increasing the risk of erosion of bare soil. Burning can also make soil particles hydrophobic (repelling water), reducing infiltration of rainfall into the soil and underlying aquifers. However, these too are natural processes and part of natural successions (changing biological community structure over time) and evolutionary processes.

A surprising number of plants are pryophytic, meaning adapted to fire. Amongst these adaptations are those species with fire-adapted seeds. The Lodgepole pine (*Pinus contorta* var. *latifolia*) is one such tree species, dominant in some North American sub-alpine forests in part due to its ability to reproduce prolifically fol-lowing wildfire. This is because some lodgepole pine cones are sealed shut by a resinous substance, remaining on the trees for a number of years and only releasing their enclosed seeds when the resin melts during forest fires. Australian forest ecosystems are also fire-adapted, in addition, *Eucalyptus* and *Banksia* trees with cones or fruits that are completely sealed with resin which is physically melted by the heat of periodic fires. The seeds of other shrubs and annual plants require chemical signals from smoke and charred plant matter to activate after a dormant period of years or decades buried in the soil seed bank, sprouting in the presence of these chemical stimuli. Other plants, such as various species of aloe and *Protea*, retain outer layers of bark, dead leaves or moist tissues, particularly around their buds, that serve as thermal insulation during fire events. Some trees, including larches and giant sequoias, have very thick, fire-retardant bark that can withstand being burned by all but the most intense fires without sustaining significant damage to their vital tissues.

Other plants, again including several species of *Eucalyptus* tree adapted to Australian dryland conditions in which wildfires are frequent, have specialised buds protected under the bark of their trunks, evolved to help them sprout new leaves and branches rapidly after the trees have been burned. A number of other plants, including some *Banksia* species and other shrubs with swollen stem bases or underground woody organs known as lignotubers as well as many herbaceous plants with fleshy bulbs, rhizomes or other underground stems, rely on these underground structures to regrow after fires even if the above-ground portion has been destroyed.

Other plants, such as the Australian grass tree (*Xanthorrhoea* species), common in the Big Desert of Victoria state, are adapted to flower prolifically after a fire such that their seeds can exploit the nutrient-rich ash and the absence of competitive vegetation. In fact, several fire lily species (*Cyrtanthus* species) only flower after fires, showing an extremely fast flowering response to natural bush fires. Still more plants, such as the stone pine (*Pinus pinea*) found in Mediterranean forests amongst other pine and many *Eucalyptus* species, have tall crowns and either few or no lower branches, such that their leaves and vital growth tissues are above the reach of all but the tallest flames.

Today, many wildfires result from human activities, both deliberate and accidental. However, lightning strikes are a common natural cause of fires, for example in the western United States and in Alaska where these meteorological conditions are prevalent. A record of historic fires can be found by interpreting scarring patterns amongst the growth rings in tree trunks.

SUSTAINABLE MANAGEMENT OF FIRE

Different ecosystems tend to burn with different frequencies and durations, affected by many factors including the type of vegetation in any given ecosystem. Man-made plantations, particularly in drier areas, tend to comprise dense plantings of smaller trees, this greater concentration of potential fuel tending to be more prone to the spread and intensity of fire. Also, fire adapted species, such as eucalyptus species, evolved in drier Australian habitats but now widespread in plantations around the world for their rapid growth, can substantially increase risk of wildfires that may spread rapidly much as they would in naturally burning Australian settings. There is a growing consensus that one of the best ways to reduce wildfire risk in forests is through the reintroduction of fire.

This may seem counter-intuitive, but an analogy could be drawn with the modern approach to flood risk management entailing encouraging flooding of upstream landscapes that formerly used to naturally flood, retaining and slowing flows of water and so reducing downstream flood peaks whilst also promoting natural floodplain functions beneficial to catchment ecology. In the case of fire, periodic burning due to either natural causes or managed ignition can control the rate of spread and severity of wildfires by reducing vegetation density, and hence fuel load. In the United States, readings of scarring patterns reveal that low-elevation forests comprising ponderosa pine (*Pinus ponderosa*) and dry Douglas fir (*Pseudotsuga menziesii*) historically had average low intensity fire intervals of 5 to 20 years, but fire suppression activities at the hands of humanity have tended to result in more intense fires due to the build-up of fuel and creation of conditions more conducive to fire hazards. Another approach with potential is 'silvicultural thinning' entailing selective removal of small-diameter trees to reduce overall tree densities, particularly closest to homes and other infrastructure.

The importance of fire for the wellbeing of some ecosystems was often not recognised in some early nature conservation strategies. A case in point here are the iconic redwood forests of California, within which some individual redwood trees (family *Sequoioideae*) are more than 2,000 years old and carry the signs of fire scarring. In the early part of the 20th century, fires in Californian coastal redwood forests were prevented or suppressed. However, the redwood forests were in decline with poor regeneration of younger trees and competition by tanoak trees (*Notholithocarpus* species). Only later, informed by observations of the ecological consequences of wildfires in this lightning-prone region, did awareness emerge that the redwood trees actually depended on periodic fires to maintain their dominance of these coastal forests.

Whilst tanoaks are themselves highly resistant to fire, the redwoods were found to be virtually indestructible. Redwood survival is enabled by a high tannin content in the bark and heartwood, not only giving the redwoods their common name but also with flame retardant properties and also protecting the trees against disease and the attentions of insects. Redwoods also have a low resin content, further reducing their flammability. In addition, the bark of mature redwood trees has a high water content and can be at least 1 foot (30 centimetres) thick, serving as a great protective shield against fires. This helps prevent fire from getting to the more easily burned sapwood behind the bark. Furthermore, as they are the world's tallest trees, most wildfires do not spread up into the tops of the trees where their broad, flat needle leaves trap moisture from the air creating drops that fall to the forest floor reducing fire ignition, spread and intensity. The conclusion of researchers was that, to retain redwood dominance in these forests, periodic fires were essential. This now informs management by state forest departments.

FIRE AND HUMAN EVOLUTION

There can be little doubt that control of the elemental force of fire was an innovation of huge significance to the technological evolution of humanity. The earliest records of the control of fire by early humanoids date from 1.7 to 0.2 million years ago, through estimates based on the analysis of microscopic traces of wood ash dating back 1.0 million years have the strongest scientific support. Evidence of the use of fire in tool manufacture is found around the early human world across subsequent time periods.

The eventual 'domestication' of fire by construction and regular fuelling of hearths may have precipitated the foundation of small communities, though this is largely speculation. What is more certain is that fire provided early humans with warmth, and hence less vulnerability to colder climates and seasons. It was also significant in warding off would-be predators, providing a source of light enabling people to be active and creative after darkness had fallen as well as perhaps signalling between settlements. It enabled greater sophistication in the manufacture of tools. It also enabled the cooking of food. Harnessing of fire to actively burn areas to promote growth of edible plants or potential fodder to attract grazing animals appears to have followed at some indeterminate stage thereafter. All of these factors would have been significant in the geographic dispersal of humans. Throughout history, fire has played deeply significant roles in our development.

The use of fire to cook food has a very long history and prehistory, and a huge probable significance in our evolution. Artefacts suggest that fire may have been used to cook food for nearly 2 million years, or perhaps even longer.[4] The everyday act of using fire, or today other controlled means of heat, to cook food is in reality far from mundane. In fact, it was a vast evolutionary step forward for humanity. The taste of cooked food is one outcome, but the liberation of digestible chemicals through the cooking of food, including increasing eating of energy-rich meat made palatable through this process, provided not only a nutritional boost but also the surplus energy necessary for the generation of the big brains that so characterise our species.

What we know from fossil records is that a doubling in the size of the brain in *Homo erectus*, considered the first modern human species, occurred over the course of 600,000 years simultaneously with these protohumans learning to cook. Primates of a similar size, such as gorillas, chimpanzees and others amongst the great apes for which the brain did not undergo such an increase in size, subsisted as they still do on a diet of raw foods.

A 2012 study measuring body and brain masses and caloric intake amongst primates perhaps unsurprisingly found a direct correlation between calories consumed and body mass.[5] A further implication of this study is that body size may be limited by the number of hours in the day available for foraging and eating, including that taken to chew through tough and fibrous plants. Energetic limits are also imposed on brain size as, weight-for-weight, brain matter expends more calories than other body tissues. As the 2012 study reports, *'Apes can't afford both brain and body'*. Neither can humans that, at some point in our evolutionary past, embarked on the route of larger brain and lesser brawn such that, today, the modern

---

[4] Wrangham, R. (2010). *Catching Fire: How Cooking Made Us Human*. Basic Books.
[5] Fonseca-Azevedo, K. and Herculano-Houzel, S. (2012). Metabolic constraint imposes tradeoff between body size and number of brain neurons in human evolution. *PNAS*, 109(45), pp. 18571–18576. DOI: https://doi.org/10.1073/pnas.1206390109.

human brain is much bigger than our body size would otherwise suggest on purely energetic grounds. Cooking may have been a key innovation on this journey, not only releasing more flavours and softening tough fibres but also allowing the meal to be metabolised completely, compared to only 30–40% of the nutrients of raw food available through digestion. If our ancestors spent less time searching for and chewing through raw food, more time and energy could be spent on other things turning our big brains from an energy drain into an asset increasing our capacities to access nutrition. Excess energetic and mental capacities enabled cascading technological, expressive and other forms of creativity, leading to the rise of cultures and behaviours.

Assumptions have been made about the rising importance of cooked food in the evolution of hominids by observing reductions in the size of the gastrointestinal tract, though we have also to be aware that the energetic efficiency of protohumans becoming bipedal may have a role to play there too. Cooking may also have played a role in the evolution of human behaviours, including the differentiation of traditional roles by sex as still widely established in cultures across the world. Also, perhaps even the deepening of pair bonding, larger and stronger men hunting and protecting the home and hearth around which women would likely have been the leading nurturing force in childbearing and childcare as well as 'home economics'.

Artefacts left in the Palaeolithic era, between 200,000 and 40,000 years before the present day, demonstrate that protohumans and early humans were constructing primitive hearths with circles of stones. These hearths featured for millennia as focal points in human homes. Indeed, the Latin word 'focus' literally means 'hearth' or 'fireplace', and modern usage of the term is believed to have entered the English language by that route as the hearth was the focal point of the home. And so almost every modern household had a fireplace up until gas became available around 150 years ago. That said, it is estimated that at least 3 billion people worldwide, approaching 40% of the global population, still cook their meals over open fires. Another interesting bit of etymology here is the origins of the word 'curfew', derived from the mediaeval 'curfew' that was derived in turn from the French 'couvre feu': a large metal cover placed over the embers of a fire during the night to keep it burning until dawn.

All of this evidence and speculation though does suggest that the new-found abilities of our ancestors to harness fire for cooking may have been significant in the rise of our species, *Homo sapiens*.

Harnessing and keeping the home fires burning may have been not only clever, but pivotal in human evolution.

FIRE IN THE SOUL

One thing we know about fire is that it is only humans that have learned to harness this amazing natural element.

Fire is captivating, capturing the imagination of cultures throughout history. Throughout our history and across all cultures, fire has represented very many things. Fire is variously recognised as a destroyer but also a purifier, an excruciating but also emblematic means of execution, as well as a regenerative power, and a symbol of change and of energy. Fire has variously been construed as warmth, light and safe harbour — hearth and home — as well as a purgative force. Fire is seen variously as a thing of dread but also of beauty, from its intense colours to its dancing flames. Spiritually, it has been imbued with meanings ranging from damnation in hell to heavenly light, of enlightenment as well as destruction, and of transfiguration. We have the mythology of the phoenix, the bird that dies in flames to be reborn, and the transfer of that archetypal human story into various religions such as the rebirth of Christ after crucifixion.

The archetypal role of fire and its elusive and transient nature has resulted, unsurprisingly, in fire gods appearing in cultures globally and throughout all of human history. Fire is deified from the Egyptian Ra (fire god of the sun, light, warmth and growth) and Sekhmet (protective lioness goddess of the sun and fire) to a range of Chinese gods of fire (Zhurong, Yandi, Ebo and Yùyōu amongst others), the Hindu Agni (god of fire, messengers and purification), the Mongolian Yal-un Eke (mother goddess of fire), Basque Eate (god of fire and storms), Greek Helios (personification of the sun), Mesopotamian Ishum (god of fire) and Māori Mahuea (goddess of fire), amongst many others. Candles and other forms of fire feature in the rituals of many global religions and associated meditations, the 'living flame' ascribed all manner of numinous qualities.

Fire also constituted a symbolic form of torture and execution. The burning of so-called heretics or of proscribed literature are dark stains in church history, famously including the French Joan of Arc (*Jeanne d'Arc*, c.1412–1431) considered a heroine of France for her role in the Hundred Years' War and later canonized as a Roman Catholic saint. However, this grizzly practice was far from limited to European Christendom. Death by burning has a long history as a form of capital punishment from parts of the law codes of Old Babylonia (18th century BC) promulgated by King Hammurabi, and of Ancient Egypt and Assyria, Hebraic law and Celtic traditions. It has featured in a wide diversity of branches of Christianity notably including the European witch-hunts of the mid-16th century, as also amongst indigenous North Americans and in some Islamic countries. Bride-burning is a still-present, albeit illegal punishment inflicted against perceived dishonourable women by some radical Hindu fundamentalists. There may be links here with the everyday English word 'bonfire', believed to have been derived from the late Middle English 'bone fire' denoting a large open-air fire on which bones were burnt, sometimes as part of a celebration but perhaps with deeper religious connotations.

Of the four elements of earth, water, air and fire, fire has served as one of the most dramatic and enduring inspirations of art. Fire has featured in cave paintings from the Palaeolithic. When the famous cave paintings of Lascaux cave, France, were discovered in 1940, more than 100 small stone lamps that had once burned grease rendered from animal fat were also found throughout the cave's various chambers. Archaeologists had assumed that they were used simply for warmth and cooking. Today, there is dawning realisation that these candles may have been strategically placed around the cave such that the narrow aura of light emitted from their flickering flames was part of a staging of the art daubed on the cave's walls and roof, as part of an unfolding story as the candles were moved. Fire has inspired art throughout history, from depictions of Prometheus — the Titan who defied the gods by stealing fire and giving it to humanity — to pre-industrial depictions of volcanoes to industrial furnaces and forges, and firework displays from ancient China to the present day. The dance of fire has served as a muse inspiring human dance or music such as Stravinsky's *The Firebird*. The candle on a dinner table is widely recognised as a romantic centrepiece.

FIRING THE IMAGINATION

Fire literally fires our imagination, so primal is it to our history and needs.

Striking a match, or lighting a candle or bonfire, may be commonplace activities. Yet, the ecology of the living element of fire — the release of long-trapped fossilised sunbeams — is anything but ordinary.

11 Glorious Mud

For some, it is just 'dirt'. For others, it 'muddies the waters'. Also, 'soiling' refers to things that are unclean. But mud in reality is marvellous, indeed nearly miraculous stuff.

Soil has myriad amazing properties, without which virtually all life on Earth — including our own — would be practically impossible.

So, what is this mysterious substance we call soil?

THE NATURE OF MUD

In the simplest of terms, soil is the name we ascribe to the massively heterogeneous brownish, reddish or black surface layer of Planet Earth. In fact, it is sometimes described as the 'skin of the earth'.

Soil is an extremely complex and regionally variable mixture of rock particles, clay and organic remains, minerals, water and air, and countless organisms both large and microscopic. Far from being inert 'dirt', soil is a living thing, every one of its constituents interacting with all other parts as a kind of amorphous 'superorganism'. We know that we grow plants in it, and that it is therefore vital for supporting higher rooted plant life. But, in reality, soil is vital for virtually all life on our home planet.

So how then did this mysterious living, amorphous mass get there in the first place?

73

The 'parent materials' forming the basis of soils derive from the gradual physical, chemical or biological weathering of different types of rock, themselves highly variable in chemical and physical properties. These parent materials are subsequently augmented by accumulation of a diverse assemblage of organic and other kinds of matter. This rich amalgam is further modified by the actions of water, wind, the effects of living organisms and the passage of time and gravity to produce a diversity of soil types.

All of these complex constituents and interactions produce a bewildering variety of soils across the Earth's surface. Soils, for example, formed from granite are often sandy, free-draining and relatively infertile, whereas those derived from the breakdown of basalt under moist conditions tend to be fertile, rich in clay and tend to retain water. Landscape topography also exerts significant influences on soil type and depth, and location affects the amount of rain that falls, the type of vegetation that grows, and the degree of exposure to water movement, gravity and wind. Soils on steep hills are usually shallower than those in valley bottoms, where sediment tends to accumulate. Soils formed in wetlands are often highly enriched with organic matter, tending to be anoxic (lacking in oxygen), which results in slow or negligible breakdown of plant matter producing peaty soils.

LIVING SOILS

Far from their ostensibly inert appearance, soils are then very much living things. They are home to a bewildering diversity of plants, fungi, bacteria, worms, ants, mites and other organisms, both visible and many more microscopic. Some live entirely within soils, whilst other organisms spend only a portion of their life cycles within the soil or on its immediate surface including in surface litter and other forms of decaying matter such as rotting logs or animal remains.

Soil biodiversity is both vital but also poorly understood. Despite our major knowledge gaps about them, soil organisms represent a large fraction of global terrestrial biodiversity. We have thus far identified only about 1% of soil microorganisms, despite knowing that they play a wide array of fundamental roles in biogeochemical and other processes vital for the continuity of life, including human wellbeing.

This wealth of soil biodiversity, and the complex food webs within it, are vital for the health and fertility of soils in both natural and agricultural ecosystems. Soil ecosystems break down wastes and recycle their essential nutrients and embedded chemical energy. Some soil surface organisms photosynthesise, converting solar energy into complex organic matter built from water and atmospheric carbon dioxide, and also therefore play important roles in climate regulation as they lock carbon into the soils they inhabit. Other soil organisms break down soil minerals and help make them available to other organisms within and growing from the soil. Highly significant amongst these are fungi, many of which are associated closely with plant roots and are known as mycorrhiza. Mycorrhiza colonise plant roots for symbiotic (or mutual) benefit: the plant gains access to minerals mobilised by fungi that, in return, receive sugars and other carbohydrates from the plant roots on or within which they live.

Other bigger beasts are also common in soils. Many of them are microfauna, less than a tenth of a millimetre in diameter, including small collembola (a group of arthropods more commonly known as springtails) and mites, protozoa and nematode worms. Nematodes, tiny elongated roundworms, are common in soils everywhere, many of them eating bacteria including potentially harmful micro-organisms, but other nematodes predate larger animals or consume plant matter. Other groups of larger mesofauna (typically between 1/10th of a millimetre and 2 millimetres in diameter) and macrofauna (larger than 2 millimetres) commonly found in soils include pseudoscorpions, larger springtails and mites, termites and ants, various larval or adult beetles, and various groups of worms including earthworms. Earthworms themselves are a diverse group of organisms that perform a range of important functions in soils, including carrying plant matter down into the soil, storing and recycling organic matter and nutrients, increasing soil porosity enabling gas exchanges and percolation of water, and influencing the availability of soil nutrients for plants. But we will consider the not so humble world of earth-worms in Chapter 18, *For the Love of Worms*.

A PRECIOUS YET VULNERABLE RESOURCE

Soil takes a staggeringly long time to form, and to build in complexity and function. As a general 'rule of thumb', highly variable with latitude, topography, climate and many other factors, just 1 inch of soil may take anything from 200 to 400 years to form. Soil formation tends to be quickest in wet tropical areas, but is far slower in cool and dry climates. However, physical formation is only part of the equation of the living nature of soil, with soil fertility taking closer to 3,000 years to fully build.

Compare this to contemporary rates of soil loss. Today's uses of agricultural land and other forms of development and activities erode soils at very rapid pace compared to its natural replenishment. Rain washes away soil through runoff over bare, tilled surfaces denuded of their natural covering of vegetation. The feet of excessive densities of livestock rob surfaces of anchoring plant roots as well as directly loosening the soil. Exposed surfaces are also subject to Aeolian (wind-transported) erosion, capable of carrying away substantial loads of soil sometimes over continental ranges. Deforestation disproportionately increases rates of soil loss, gullies forming particularly on sloping land from which canopy cover and an-choring roots have been removed. Globally, it is estimated that human activities have increased the rate at which erosion would naturally occur by 10–50 times. This depletes the fundamental resource vital for the food security of a growing global human population.

For soil, as for water, mined substances, atmospheric chemistry, fisheries and other aspects of biodiversity, we are effectively depleting the non-renewable stock upon which future wellbeing depends in pursuit of short-term goals. This trajectory does not promise a happy ending for our future security and prospects for living fulfilled lives.

DIAMONDS IN THE DIRT

What if we truly valued the underappreciated 'diamonds in the dirt'? The often-ignored resource of soil grows much of our food, we build houses, industrial and other infrastructure on it, and it forms the basis for valued and aesthetic landscapes. Soils retain more water than that which is visible in surface freshwater pools and streams. They also host purification processes, buffer extreme water flows playing significant roles in reducing risks of flooding and droughts, and promote replenishment of groundwater. Soils also interact with the atmosphere, air-filled pores accounting for typically around 25% of soil volume. They play fundamental roles in planetary cycles of water, nutrients and carbon. (The world's soils cumulatively store more carbon than that contained in the atmosphere and all plant and animal life combined).

Adverse consequences also arise when soil ends up in the wrong place, silting river and sea beds and carrying with it nutrient and other substances that severely damage receiving ecosystems. Accelerated soil loss also represents the squandering of an essential, inherently renewable yet incredibly slowly formed primary resource vital for managing future food security, flood and drought regulation, natural beauty, stable foundations besides many more benefits.

We overlook the value or lose 'diamonds in the dirt' at our considerable peril.

12 What's So Special about Fish?

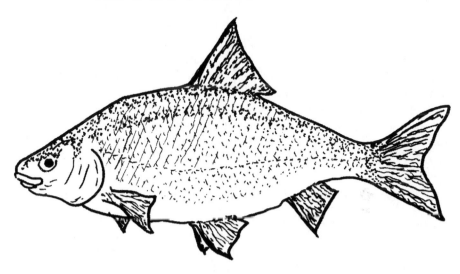

Apart from encountering them cooked in batter on our plates, as a calming presence in a tank in the dentist's waiting room or spotting one finning in a river below a town bridge, perhaps most of us give fish little second thought. Some people think about them far more frequently, of course, including anglers, commercial fishermen and aquaculturalists, and pet fish hobbyists. But fish actually do a surprisingly diverse number of things that are ultimately beneficial to us.

DIRECT USES OF FISH

Many of us enjoy eating fish from time to time. However, for many people, they are an essential protein source. In fact, fish form an important element of the global human food supply, accounting for roughly one-fifth of all animal protein in the human diet. Capture fisheries and aquaculture provide 3 billion people globally with almost 20% of their average per capita intake of animal protein, and a further 1.3 billion people with about 15%, though this share can reach 50% in some countries and 60% of more in west Africa and south Asia, with global fish production exceeding that of poultry, beef or pork.[1] Asia accounts for almost two-thirds of global fish consumption. An estimated 120 million people worldwide work in the capture fisheries sector and its supply chains; half of them are women, so these fishery activities also make a significant contribution to gender equality, financial security and allied livelihoods. The financial value of

---

[1] Williams, M. (1996). *The Transition in the Contribution of Living Aquatic Resources to Food Security, Food, Agriculture, and the Environment.* Discussion Paper 13 International Food Policy Research Institute, Washington, DC, pp. 3–24.

global fisheries is elusive given the substantial volumes of fish serving subsistence needs, but the value of global fish exports in 2017 stood at $US152 billion, 54% of produce originating from developing countries.[2]

In addition to their value as a food source, the sale of tradable stock fish[3] and the substantial international trade in ornamental fish[4] are also of significant value to society, both economically as well as in supporting livelihoods and lifestyles. Fish are also put to a diversity of other local uses. These uses include, as some amongst many examples, oil extraction, fertiliser, feed for stock animals, ornamental resources and a range of other applications. One amazing instance is the eulachon (*Thaleichthys pacificus*) of the Pacific coast of North America, a fish that contains so much body fat during spawning — up to 15% of body mass — that the dried fish can be strung on a wick and burned as a candle.[5] Other fish parts are put to diverse human uses, including the sharp and tough scales of the arapaima (fishes of the genus *Arapaima*) from Amazonia which are used as arrowheads, and the very large scales of the mahseer (fishes of the genus *Tor*) in India used as dinner plates or various forms of decoration.

THE ROLES OF FISH IN REGULATING THE ENVIRONMENT

Some species of fish play important roles in the regulation of diseases. This occurs naturally, with fish eating and controlling the numbers of snails, water fleas, mosquito larvae and a range of other aquatic organisms that serve as vectors in the spread of waterborne parasites and diseases responsible for serious conditions such as malaria, bilharzia, river blindness, Rift Valley fever, West Nile virus, guinea worm and many more. People have exploited 'mosquito fish' widely for the control of the larvae of the mosquito vectors of malaria across the tropics. The term 'mosquito fish' covers a range of fish species, particularly livebearers (a family of fish that release free-swimming young rather than laying eggs), particularly including the guppy (*Poecilia reticulata*) and also *Gambusia affinis*. These fish have consequently been introduced to control mosquito larvae in tropical water bodies, though the effectiveness of their introduction for this purpose is subject to some uncertainty.[6]

Before public water systems were developed in the 1960s in outlying regions of Sweden, it was also common practice to drop eels (*Anguilla anguilla*) into household wells to control bugs, flies and other pests. One of these eels lived an abnormally long life of 155 years, the world's oldest recorded age for an eel after its

---

[2] FAO. (2018). *The State of World Fisheries and Aquaculture 2018 — Meeting the Sustainable Development Goals*. Food and Agriculture Organization (FAO), Rome. (http://www.fao.org/3/i9540en/i9540en.pdf, accessed 26 May 2020.)

[3] Everard M. (2009). *Ecosystem Services Case Studies*. Environment Agency Science Report SCHO0409BPVM-E-E. Environment Agency, Bristol.

[4] Bartley, D. (2005). *Fisheries and Aquaculture Topics. Ornamental Fish*. Topics Fact Sheets. UN Food and Agriculture Organization (FAO), Fisheries and Aquaculture Department, Rome. (http://www.fao.org/fishery/topic/13611/en, accessed 26 May 2020.)

[5] Everard, M. (2012). *Fantastic Fishes: A Feast of Fishy Facts and Fables*. Medlar Press: Ellesmere.

[6] Chandra, G., Bhattacharjee, I., Chatterjee S.N. and Ghosh, A. (2008). Mosquito control by larvivorous fish. *Indian Journal of Medical Research*, 127, pp. 13–27.

death in 2017.[7] This venerable eel had occupied the same family well since Napoleon III was King of France and work had just started on the Suez Canal, enduring two world wars but regarded as a family pet throughout much of its later life. This record eel is survived by another in the same well believed to be a more youthful 110 years old.

However, fish can also be vectors of some other parasites affecting wildlife (as discussed in Chapter 9, *Unappealing Creatures*) as well as some also potentially infecting humans when uncooked fish are eaten. The management and use of fish stocks therefore needs careful consideration.

Fish have also had a significant influence on the ways in which people manage the quality of the water environment, including both retaining the natural purification processes of freshwater ecosystems as well as the legislation, technologies and investments deployed to manage pollution. The needs of freshwater fish populations have for many years formed the basis for quality standards used for water quality management, including the European Union (EU) Freshwater Fish Directive[8] which, in 1978, became one of the EU's first pieces of environmental legislation. (The EU Freshwater Fish Directive has since been repealed and its requirements subsumed within the EU Water Framework Directive.) There is also a rich case law under common law relating to freshwater fisheries,[9] reflecting the importance of maintaining fish populations for a diversity of public interests.

However, the presence of the wrong type of fish can also present problems for the maintenance of ecosystem balances and quality, with adverse consequences for people. Typically, this occurs when fish species have been introduced into places in which they are not native, and so are no longer subject to the 'checks and balances' of other organisms with which they have co-evolved. A globally widespread example is the common carp (*Cyprinus carpio*), a sediment-grubbing species of freshwater fish native to the Black and Caspian Sea basins that is highly efficient at converting a diversity of food resources into carp protein. For this reason, it has been spread to all continents, where it has often severely perturbed the balance of native ecosystems damaging wildlife and water resources. It is not without good reason that I have described common carp as 'pigs with fins' in two of my other books,[10,11] a descriptor that has not automatically endeared me to all of my angling buddies! A wide range of other non-native fish species, introduced deliberately or as accidental releases from aquaculture, the pet fish trade or by angling interests, have become invasive and caused formerly unforeseen and not infrequently adverse outcomes for ecosystems and people.

---

[7] The Telegraph. (2017). Swedish eel slithers its last after 155 years. *The Telegraph*, 6 November 2017. (https://www.telegraph.co.uk/news/worldnews/europe/sweden/11023470/Swedish-eel-slithers-its-last-after-155-years.html, accessed 26 May 2020.)

[8] CEC. (1978). *Directive on the Quality of Fresh Waters Needing Protection or Improvement in Order to Support Fish Life*. 78/659/EEC.

[9] Carty P. and Payne S. (1998). *Angling and the Law*. Merlin Unwin Books: Ludlow, UK.

[10] Everard, M. (2012). *Fantastic Fishes: A Feast of Fishy Facts and Fables*. Medlar Press: Ellesmere.

[11] Everard, M. (2020). *The Complex Lives of British Freshwater Fishes*. CRC Press/Taylor & Francis: Boca Raton, FL.

FISH ENRICH OUR LIVES

Fish also play major roles, sometimes valued but far more frequently overlooked, in the enrichment of human societies.

Some degree of quantification of the extent to which fishery ecosystems can define the cultures, traditions and economy of communities and whole societies has become evident through various substantial legal cases taken when those fish stocks were damaged or expunged. Just one example, in this instance associated with sizeable legal reparations to the affected community, is that of the Grand Coulee Dam in the United States. When the Grand Coulee Dam was developed progressively between 1933 and 1955 for hydropower generation and irrigation supply, impacts on the migration of fish, particularly native species of Pacific salmon, and the consequences for the livelihoods of upstream native American and Canadian First Nations people were inadequately considered. Yet, production of salmon and other fish had been the centrepiece of the area's indigenous culture, identity and economy. In 1951, the Colville Confederated Tribes filed a suit against the United States for damages caused by loss of the fish populations that had shaped their culture. The Indian Claims Commission ruled in 1978, 27 years after the claim had been filed, that the tribes were entitled to full compensation for all income losses associated with the dam, for which the US government provided in total US$66 million as historic compensation including annual payments of US$15 million to offset ongoing reduced income opportunities. Damage to the traditions and culture of the Confederated Tribes was in fact irreparable, and also inadequately substituted by monetary payments alone, yet the substantial sums involved give some indication of the importance of the natural cycles of salmon and other native fishes to tribal culture.

The Japanese are of course closely associated with their marine environment and its stocks of fish and other resources. Owing to the steep topography of much of the interior of the islands of Japan and its extremely dense human population, one of the world's densest particularly in clusters around the coasts, fish feature heavily in the nation's myth, symbolism, culture and diet. Just one of many signals of the importance of fish to Japanese culture are the prices paid recently for the sale of tuna. Staggeringly, a single bluefin tuna weighing in at 269 kg (593 lb) sold at market for a record three quarters of a million US dollars (56.49 m Yen, $US736,000, £472,125) at the first auction of 2012 in Tokyo's Tsukiji fish market, a price almost double that paid the previous year.[12] The winning bidder, self-styled 'Tuna King' Kiyoshi Kimura, was the owner of a sushi restaurant chain. This highlighted the extent to which the flesh of the tuna is prized. More amazingly, the same restaurateur paid a new record 155 m Yen (US$1.7 m; £1.05 m) for a single bluefin tuna weighing in at 222 kg (489 lb) in 2013, nearly tripling the record of the previous year.[13] Even more amazingly, he surpassed himself again in 2019 by paying a record US$3.1 m (£2.5 m) for a giant 278 kg (612 lb) bluefin tuna during the first new year's auction in Tokyo's new fish market.[14] Whilst part of this high

---

[12] http://www.bbc.co.uk/news/world-asia-pacific-16421231, accessed 26 May 2020.

[13] http://www.bbc.co.uk/news/world-asia-20919306, accessed 26 May 2020.

[14] BBC. (2019). Japan sushi tycoon pays record tuna price. *BBC News*, 5 January 2019. (https://www.bbc.co.uk/news/world-asia-46767370, accessed 26 May 2020.)

price is undoubtedly related to marketing for the restaurant owner, it also reflects both the esteem in which tuna sushi is held as well as the increasing scarcity of these magnificent and charismatic oceanic predators.

Although market prices are poor substitutes for the wider benefits provided to people by ecosystems and the species they contain, they do at least give us some sense of the scale of value at least for those organisms that have gastronomic, recreational or other utilitarian uses. For example, koi carp — the shortened and better-known version of the Japanese word *nishikigoi* (translating as 'brocaded carp') — are prized highly in Japan and elsewhere in the world for their vivid colours. They are considered a form of living art, for which they have been se-lectively bred and reared for centuries. Koi are ubiquitous in Japanese culture, from art to fishponds, cuisine, kites and tattoos. High status is attached to owning the finest fish, and koi are also symbolic of long life and prosperity. In 2010, the record price paid by a UK collector for a single koi was £100,000 for a specimen, though particularly strikingly patterned koi can sell for as much as £500,000 elsewhere in the world.[15] The prices and possession of the finest koi in Japan are closely guarded secrets by their owners, though it reputed that the most expensive koi carp ever sold fetched a staggering \$US2.2 million.[16]

Recreational fisheries are also of significant cultural and associated economic importance, and again the sums involved are substantial. For example, the UK's Sports Council estimated annual spend by anglers in the UK at £1.2 billion (excluding VAT),[17] whilst the National Rivers Authority concluded in 1994 that there were 2.9 million freshwater and sea anglers in England and Wales, who spent £3.3 billion per annum.[18] Values for Scotland are also substantial, a Scottish Government estimate reckoning that each rod-caught salmon represents £2,500 of value to the Scottish economy and that the value to Scotland of angling is over £120 million per year compared to the far lower value of the Scottish salmon netting industry of £1.75 million.[19] The angling tourism industry is also reported to be worth a bare minimum of €66 million to the Republic of Ireland.[20] Across the UK, the Labour Party's 'Charter for Angling'[21] estimated annual spend on angling at £5 billion. Further health and lifestyle benefits are known to accrue from the activities of angling

---

[15] http://www.thisismoney.co.uk/money/investing/article-1679650/How-to-invest-and-make-money-from-Koi-carp.html, accessed 26 May 2020.

[16] http://molometer.hubpages.com/hub/Koi-Carp-An-Ancient-Long-Lived-Ornamental-Fish, accessed 26 May 2020.

[17] Sports Council. (1991). *Angling — An Independent Review*. UK Sports Council: London.

[18] National Rivers Authority. (1994). *National Angling Survey 1994*. Fisheries Technical Report No.5. National Rivers Authority, Bristol.

[19] Association of Salmon Fishery Boards, Atlantic Salmon Trust and Salmon and Trout Association. (2009). *Threats from, and Practical Solutions to, Scottish Coastal Mixed Stock Salmon Fisheries.* Paper submitted by Association of Salmon Fishery Boards, Atlantic Salmon Trust and Salmon and Trout Association on 9 February 2009 to the Scottish Government, MSFWG0905. (http://www.scotland.gov.uk/Resource/Doc/1063/0079467.pdf, accessed 26 May 2020.)

[20] Fine Gael Tourism spokesperson is quoted in EFTTA. (2009). EFTTA backs MEP on sea fishing. *NewsLines: News for the European Fishing Tackle Trade,* January 2009. European Fishing Tackle Trade Association. pp. 2–3.

[21] Salter M. (2005). *Labour's Charter for Angling 2005*. Labour Party: London.

and other related outdoor pursuits, although these have not been costed.[22] Angling for freshwater fish also generates social cohesion, not merely though angling clubs and the infrastructure supplying angling equipment, accommodation and hospitality, but in its potential role in combating social exclusion and as a significant means to draw younger people away from anti-social behaviour.[23] Angling participation is also high in the UK, involving some 3.8 million freshwater anglers, representing 9% of the adult population, with a further 8% 'very' or 'quite' interested in angling.[24,25]

However, reducing fish down to crude financial sums, however staggeringly large, is wholly inadequate to express the range and depth of their importance to humanity. This includes their utility but also the very many things that they do within ecosystems from which we benefit.

One particularly interesting use to which we put fish is at the forefront of the 'war on terror'. In the United States, fish are used in counter-terrorism measures, particularly in the post-9/11 homeland security response following attacks on the World Trade Center in Lower Manhattan, New York.[26,27] As terrorist poisoning of municipal water supplies is of high concern, fish have been deployed since 2006 in terror warning systems in San Francisco, New York, Washington, DC and some other major American cities. The fish are placed in holding tanks flushed continuously by water abstracted for municipal water supply, playing the metaphorical role of 'canaries in a coal mine' as their sensitivity to minute levels of toxins is far more immediate and acute than laboratory test equipment. Sophisticated video and behavioural models monitor the breathing, heartbeat and swimming patterns of these fish around the clock, automatically triggering electronic warnings of possible contamination of the water supply. There are documented reports of at least one instance of the system intercepting a toxin, albeit not terrorism related, before it got out of control and contaminated the public water supply serving New York City, the fish responding to contamination traces 2 hours earlier than they were picked up by other detection devices in use by the city's Department of Environmental Protection. Interestingly, online documentation of this use of fishes has largely disappeared from the internet over recent years.

Many freshwater fish species are also of direct conservation concern,[28] and freshwater habitats and ecosystems are amongst the most steeply declining ecosystems across the world disproportionately affected by the cumulative pressure of human activities and indicating a commensurate reduction in their capacities to support human

[22] Sport England. (2004). *The Framework for Sport in England — Making England an Active and Successful Sporting Nation: A Vision for 2020.* Sport England: London.

[23] Environment Agency. (2009). *Creating a Better Place: Environment Agency Corporate Strategy 2010–2015.* Environment Agency: Bristol. (https://www.gov.uk/government/uploads/system/uploads/attachment_data/file/288543/geho0211btkv-e-e.pdf, accessed 26 May 2020.)

[24] Environment Agency. (2001). *Public Attitudes to Angling.* Environment Agency: Bristol.

[25] Simpson D. and Mawle G.W. (2005). *Public Attitudes to Angling 2005.* Environment Agency: Bristol.

[26] Everard, M. (2012). *Fantastic Fishes: A Feast of Fishy Facts and Fables.* Medlar Press: Ellesmere.

[27] Everard, M. (2020). *The Complex Lives of British Freshwater Fishes.* CRC Press/Taylor & Francis: Boca Raton, FL.

[28] Helfman G.S. (2007). *Fish Conservation: A Guide to Understanding and Restoring Global Aquatic Biodiversity and Fishery Resources.* Island Press: Washington, DC.

wellbeing.[29] As a regional example, in 2007, 200 (38%) of the 522 European fresh-water fish species were assessed as threatened with extinction, with a further 12 already extinct, representing a greater threat than for Europe's birds or mammals.[30] Globally, approximately 20% of the world's 10,000 described freshwater fish species have been listed as threatened, endangered or extinct in the last few decades.[31] Fish populations serve as a primary indicator of the vulnerability of freshwater systems, and their capacity not merely to support fish but also to cater for human needs now and into the future. Fishes also play a role in the life cycles of many other animals, some of high conservation concern, within the ecosystems they occupy, as one example in nour-ishing, protecting and distributing the larvae of freshwater mussels.

Fish, both directly and as elements of the environments that support them, can also attract substantial ecotourism markets. Ecotourism values may exceed the regional economic value of agricultural production in the UK.[32] Fish-related tourism can also constitute a substantial element of international tourism in some regions, where the market for recreational exploitation of fish stocks can be reinvested in the community as an effective incentive for local action to conserve threatened fish stocks, associated ecosystems and the many benefits they provide to people.[33]

Freshwater fishes and the ecosystems in which they occur can also inspire and connect people with nature. Fish, for example, feature regularly in TV and radio broadcasting (such as the BBC's popular prime time *Springwatch* series in the UK) as well as literature (a well-known example is Henry Williamson's 1936 book *Salar the Salmon*[34]). Fish and fishing have also inspired music, including classical works such as Franz Schubert's *Die Forelle*[35] and many more popular songs.[36] Many prominent and charismatic fish species, such as Atlantic salmon (*Salmo salar*), are a focus for art and crafts. Also, so too are less charismatic species such as roach,[37] dace[38] and the many 'tiddlers': the smaller fish species of British fresh waters.[39]

Cultural appreciation of fish as prominent and characteristic species within fresh-water ecosystems can also provide a focus for public and organisational mobilisation around conservation projects. For example, the Thames Salmon Trust was established as a registered charity in 1986, today reconstituted as the Thames Rivers Trust, with the

[29] Millennium Ecosystem Assessment. (2005). *Ecosystem and Human Well-Being: General Synthesis.* Island Press: Vancouver.

[30] Kottelat M. and Freyhof J. (2007). *Handbook of European Freshwater Fishes.* Publications Kottelat: Cornol (Switzerland). ISBN 978-2-8399-0298-4, 2007, xiv+646 pp.

[31] Millennium Ecosystem Assessment. (2005b). *Ecosystems and Human Well-Being: Wetlands and Water — Synthesis.* World Resources Institute: Washington, DC.

[32] Everard M. (2004). Investing in Sustainable Catchments. *Science of the Total Environment,* 324(1–3), pp. 1–24.

[33] Everard M. and Kataria G. (2011). Recreational angling markets to advance the conservation of a reach of the Western Ramganga River, India. *Aquatic Conservation: Marine and Freshwater Ecosystems,* 21(1), pp. 101–108.

[34] Williamson H. (1935). *Salar the Salmon.* Faber and Faber: London.

[35] 'The Trout': A lied Op. 32 (D.550) written in 1817.

[36] Everard, M. (2012). *Fantastic Fishes: A Feast of Fishy Facts and Fables.* Medlar Press: Ellesmere.

[37] Everard, M. (2006). *The Complete Book of the Roach.* Medlar Press: Ellesmere, p. 436.

[38] Everard, M. (2011a). *Dace: The Prince of the Stream.* Calm Productions: Romford, p. 248.

[39] Everard, M. (2008). *The Little Book of Little Fishes.* Medlar Press: Ellesmere, p. 192.

ambitious aim of bringing about regeneration of the river such that salmon and migratory trout could return.[40] Like many of the UK's Rivers Trusts, an effective network of voluntary non-profit, river-focused organisations across the country often with concern for native fish stocks close to their core rationale, the Thames Rivers Trust operates largely by coordinating and focusing the limited and often discipline-centred investments of statutory regulators, local authorities and voluntary groups on the integrity of river systems. Similar examples of Rivers Trust activities are seen throughout the British Isles, with fish often serving as iconic organisms that help focus effort and indicate success in enhancing river system health and social cohesion. Consequently, a wide range of river restoration schemes, from local reaches to whole catchments, has been successfully implemented across the UK and indeed across the world. These measures improve prospects for fish and other wildlife, but also a linked set of wider societal benefits including natural management of flood risk, provision of amenity, a focus for waterfront regeneration and uplift of adjacent property values and the general enhancement of the urban environment.[41–43]

Fish swimming serenely in the tank in the dentist's waiting room, in a koi pond, in a Zen garden or in a home aquarium or garden pond bring us tranquillity. We can gaze at them for hours, particularly when we are most in need of distraction. These fish are the subject of a substantial and lucrative, global trade. In Britain, there are 2.7 million indoor fish tanks (6% households) and 1.3 million outdoor ponds supporting a pet food market worth £67 million.[44] In the United States, 10% of the population had freshwater pet fish and 2% had saltwater fish in 2016 with a combined fish food market valued at $US 142 million.[45] It seems that we have a subconscious need to find room for fish and the environments that support them in our daily lives.

THE ROLE OF FISH IN ECOSYSTEM BALANCE

Fish also play important roles in all levels of freshwater food webs, from the top predator level down to those fish species that are adapted to graze on algae. Fish thereby make important connections within ecosystems that maintain cycles of energy, nutrients and other matter. They consequently play crucial and often under-appreciated roles in maintaining nature's productivity, resilience and provision of wide-ranging benefits to humanity.

---

[40] Thames Rivers Restoration Trust. (2006). *Report and Financial Statements, Year Ended: 31 March 2006 (Charity no: 295138)*. Thames Rivers Restoration Trust: Newbury.

[41] Petts G., Heathcoate J. and Martin D. (2002). *Urban Rivers: Our Inheritance and Future*. IWA Publishing and Environment Agency: London.

[42] Petts J. (2006). Managing public engagement to optimise learning: reflections from urban river restoration. *Human Ecology Review*, 13, pp. 172–181.

[43] Everard M. (2013). *The Hydropolitics of Dams: Engineering or Ecosystems?* Zed Books: London.

[44] PFMA. (2020). *2019 Annual Report*. Pet Food Manufacturers' Association (PFMA). (https://www.pfma.org.uk/_assets/docs/annual-reports/PFMA-2019-Annual-Report.pdf, accessed 26 May 2020.)

[45] APPA. (2018). *APPA National Pet Owners Survey 2017–2018*. American Pet Products Manufacturers Association (APPMA). (https://www.americanpetproducts.org/, accessed 26 May 2020.)

As such, the diversity and abundance of geographically representative fish species can serve, and are used, as indicators of the overall health of aquatic ecosystems,[46] and by extension their resilience and capacity to serve human needs into the future.

MORE THAN JUST THINGS SERVED IN BATTER

So, all in all, there is rather more to the humble fish than what we might see served up on a plate, swimming in a tank in the corner of the dentist's waiting room, or idling in the flow beneath a town bridge. The contributions that fish and the aquatic ecosystems of which they are integral parts make to our continuing health, wealth and quality of life are as diverse as they are substantial. And, of course, all of these benefits are intimately interconnected. So, the way we use fish stocks and the water environments in which they live have to be considered carefully if we are not to perturb their delicate balances, stability and capacities to cater for our needs into the future.

Few fishes arouse great emotion amongst the general public, nor do they generally have an appeal that can rival charismatic organisms such as birds.[47] Nevertheless, as we have seen in the preceding pages, some fishes have extraordinarily high cultural significance or have served as charismatic emblems mobilising the energies of organisations and their individual members. Significant press profile has greeted the return of salmon to rivers in England's former northern industrial heartland, such as the Mersey and Don catchments, that had previously suffered from gross pollution and frequent impoundments blocking fish passage. An equivalent status for certain charismatic fishes, generally top predators and frequently migratory species, is seen across the globe, including, for example, salmon and trout in the northern temperate regions, sturgeon from central Europe, mahseer from Asia, and alligator gar from North America.

We have to take care of conflicts in the ways in which we exploit or manage fish stocks. For example, destructive commercial and subsistence fishing methods and overharvesting of fish can impose significant pressures on fishery ecosystems and the diverse benefits that they provide, as can unsympathetic aquaculture practices. We have also to be mindful of potential conflicts in the use and management of surrounding landscapes, which substantially shape the character of aquatic ecosystems and their fish stocks.

But, above all, we need to recognise that fish matter, and not solely for people who like on occasion to eat them, go fishing for them or keep them as pets. The presence of thriving fish populations assures us that our water environment is in good health. Fish form important connections in ecosystems, are ascribed cultural and economic values, provide a focal point for societies, manage transmission of some important waterborne diseases, and enrich our lives in many other ways.

All in all, fish are pretty special!

---

[46] Everard, M. (2012). *Fantastic Fishes: A Feast of Facts and Fables*. Medlar Press: Ellesmere.

[47] The UK's Royal Society for the Protection of Birds (www.RSPB.org.uk) has in excess of 1 million members.

13 Grasping the Nettle

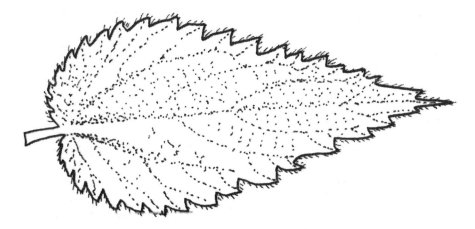

OK, I get the point that not everyone loves the humble stinging nettle, *Utica dioica*. I mainly do, apart from when I settle down on a springtime riverbank and inadvertently sit on a young plant when its string is not only most potent, but also self-inflicted on tender parts of my body. But I can forgive the nettles for this, the lack of caution being mine and that after decades of repeating the same folly! It is, in fact, a small price to pay for all the marvellous things that stinging nettles do.

To the stinging nettle, we can add a range of other 'unappealing plants' — bindweed in particular is seen as a menace amongst the gardening community — mirroring the 'unappealing creatures' we have already visited in terms of our lack of appreciation of the diversity of amazing and useful things they actually do. But, for this chapter and purpose, let's focus just on the much-maligned stinging nettle.

In our common parlance, we even have the phrase 'grasping the nettle', a figure of speech known wherever *Urtica dioica* commonly occurs and across a variety of languages. Simply, it means to brace oneself to be brave and do something that is unpleasant, or perhaps difficult. Grabbing a nettle incautiously, a bit like sitting on one on a riverbank particularly when wearing shorts, is after all not always a pleasant experience! To be 'nettled', meaning angry or irritated, also derives from the properties of this plant.

KNOWING NETTLES

The stinging nettle is also known as the common nettle — also regionally as the burn nettle, burn weed or burn hazel — and common it is too. Favouring disturbed ground and high levels of nitrogen and other nutrient substances in the soil, it is often found close to human habitation, including in farmed land. Nettles grow particularly lush around sewage works, as they did on old 'sewage farms' before they were phased out in the UK, and also livestock slurry stores where nitrogen is available in great abundance.

The plant's sting is the feature from which the stinging nettle is best known, the genus name *Urtica* in fact meaning 'sting' in Latin. (The species name *dioica* reflects that the plant is dioecious — having both male and female plants — derived from the Greek word meaning 'of two houses'.) The nettles — plants in the family Urticaceae — are perennial flowering plants. The stinging nettle was originally native to most or all of Europe and of temperate Asia as well as western North Africa. However, it has since been spread through human activity and is now widespread worldwide including, for example, in New Zealand and North America. Whilst stinging nettles can grow in stands up to 2 metres tall by late summer, the shoots die down to their spreading rhizomes (root structures) and stolons (ground-level or underground shoots) to overwinter, shoots sprouting again from early spring.

Both the leaves and stems are hairy, some hairs non-stinging but some with tips that break off when touched. These act like needles, injecting several chemicals — histamine, serotonin and choline amongst them — into exposed skin, causing the painful and characteristic sting. The sting itself is not dangerous but it is irritating, producing a burning, stinging sensation and an inflammatory effect on the skin known as 'contact urticaria'. This can be treated by various proprietary creams, particularly those containing antihistamines or hydrocortisone. However, a traditional remedy, and one with which many of us will have become familiar as children, is rubbing a dock leaf onto the affected area. Dock plants — broad-leaved plants of the genus *Rumex* and in particular the broad-leaved dock *Rumex obtusifolius* — fortunately also grow well on exactly the same kind of disturbed ground favoured by stinging nettle plants, and so are usually found growing in close proximity.

NETTLES AND NATURE

Nettles can form dense stands in the summer, upon which a number of animals feed. Notable amongst these are the larvae of a range of British and north European butterfly species, whose primary host food plant is the stinging nettle. These include the peacock butterfly (*Aglais io*), the small tortoiseshell (*Aglais urticae* the species name of which even reflects its association with nettles), the red admiral (*Vanessa atalanta*) and the comma (*Polygonia c-album*). Stinging nettles also serve as food plants for the larvae many moth species, including the angle shade (*Phlogophora meticulosa*), buff ermine (*Spilarctia luteum*) and the lesser broad-bordered yellow underwing (*Noctua janthina*). The larva of the ghost moth (*Hepialus humuli*) feeds on the roots of the stinging nettle.

Stinging nettles are particularly found as an understory plant in wetter environments, but are also found in meadows. Although nutritious, nettles are not widely eaten by either wildlife or livestock, presumably because of the sting.

The dense network of rhizomes and underground or soil-surface stolons of the stinging nettle can be important in stabilising soils that would otherwise be bare as herbaceous vegetation dies back in the winter, also trapping sediment and organic matter and thus contributing to soil formation. Owing to this rich soil surface and subsoil layer, nettle beds can host an abundance of small invertebrate life. Consequently, even on a barren, frost-wracked riverbank in December or January, you can often observe wrens and other overwintering birds probing amongst nettle stubble for a meal. The abundant seeds, and the network of rhizomes and stolons, also enable nettles to survive adverse conditions, including floods, droughts and fire, re-establishing quickly after above-ground growth is decimated and so maintaining ground cover, habitat and microclimate.

Rooting around within nettle beds — I accept you have to be a bit weird to do that but I do it nonetheless — you will be amazed how much biodiversity you find there. Spiders, earwigs, woodlice, harvestmen, aphids, slugs, snails and many more small creatures form a minute and microscopic menagerie that is far from lost on the hosts of birds that come to forage for invertebrate food. Overwintering insects can be attracted in significant numbers to fresh spring stinging nettles, which provide early food both for herbivores but also for the carnivores that feed upon them. Aphids, for example, can proliferate early in the year on stinging nettles and, in turn, provide a rich spring food source for wasps, ladybirds, blue tits and other woodland birds that can be seen foraging around nettle beds and stems. Nettle beds also play host to a wide range of predators and parasites that can spread out to provide valuable pest control services in adjacent crops and other cultivated plants. For this reason, aggressive control of nettles as 'weeds' can be counterproductive for farmers and gardeners alike in removing controls on pest infestations. The same rule also applies for various pollinating organisms that find refuge and food in nettle beds.

In addition to birds foraging on insects within nettle beds, many other larger organisms also benefit from stinging nettles. Amongst them are seed-eating birds, including, for example, goldfinches, house sparrows, chaffinches and bullfinches, that feast on the wealth of seeds that nettles produce in late summer. Hedgehogs, shrews, frogs, toads and other insect- and mollusc-eating animals also find both refuge and food in the moist microclimate within nettle beds at all times of the year.

Other plants also benefit from the activities of stinging nettles. Nettles act as 'dynamic accumulators', a term describing those plants that gather a range of mineral and nutrient substances from the soil, storing them and converting them into more bioavailable forms benefitting other plants. Nettle beds also blanket soil surfaces, retaining moisture and reducing evaporation and, as their aerial parts die back and are integrated into the soil by other organisms, they also sequester carbon into the soil thereby contributing in their small way to global climate regulation.

EATING THE NETTLE

Perhaps counterintuitively, nettles are edible. In fact, I used to eat a fair quantity of nettles at one point. They are best steamed to produce a sting-free vegetable that looks and tastes very much like spinach. Thus softened, nettles can also be turned into a puree, and also used to make pesto. Another common use of the plant is nettle soup, particularly in Northern and Eastern Europe. Used fresh or dried, the leaves and also the flowers of the stinging nettle can be used to make herbal tea. Nettles are rich in iron and other mineral elements, as well as in vitamins A and C. However, young nettles are the best, not merely as they are less stringy than old plants but also as gritty particles called cystoliths can form as the plant ages, and these can not only result in a less pleasant texture, but may also be an internal irritant.

Another culinary use of stinging nettles is in cheesemaking. They are used to wrap Cornish Yarg, a semi-hard cow's milk cheese made in Cornwall. The recipe is thought to date back to 1615, but has since been popularised by Alan and Jenny Gray who found the recipe: 'Yarg' is 'Gray' spelled backwards. Nettles are also used as a flavouring in some varieties of Gouda cheese. Stinging nettles feature as well as part of traditional dough fillings popular in Albania and Greece. Beer can also be made from young nettle leaves.

Stinging nettles can be added to the feed of laying hens, the high concentrations of carotenoids in the leaves serving as a natural pigment deepening the colour of egg yolks. Furthermore, although ruminants avoid eating fresh stinging nettles, wilted or dry plants, as also nettle silage, are palatable and of high nutritional value

However, the uses of nettles extend well beyond their values in food production. Stinging nettles have traditionally been used as a medicinal herb in Austria, prepared as a tea or else as fresh leaves to help treat kidney, urinary tract, gastro-intestinal, skin and cardiovascular conditions. In Anglo-Saxon Britain, stinging nettles were also thought to promote lactation. Furthermore, urtication — flogging or otherwise rubbing with nettles to provoke skin inflammation — was once a folk remedy to address fatigue or improve circulation. It is also alleged that Roman soldiers used to rub nettles into their skin to help them adapt to the colder, harsher climate of Britain.

The various nutritional and medicinal uses of stinging nettles have some basis in science. Mature nettle leaves are rich in α-linolenic acid, a valuable omega-3 acid, as well as a range of vitamins including vitamin A (retinol), vitamin C (ascorbic acid) and vitamin B_2 (riboflavin), and carotenoid pigments that are precursors of vitamin C.

USING THE NETTLE

People have found many uses for the humble stinging nettle other than for edible and medicinal purposes.

Ancient nettle textiles used for clothing have been found amongst Bronze Age remains in Denmark dating back almost 3,000 years. However, use of nettle-derived fabrics has a far less remote history. During World War I, 1914–1918, the uniforms of the German army were almost all made from stinging nettles, driven largely by a shortage of cotton but also as they make durable fabric. In fact, today, there are companies in Austria and Germany as well as Italy that have started to produce commercial textiles from stinging nettles.

Stinging nettles have many properties making them suitable for making fabric, despite a somewhat variable fibre content that is nonetheless comparable with that of flax stems. Nettle stems contain a harder, outer layer of bast fibre, also known as phloem fibre or skin fibre, comprising largely the stem's fluid-conducting cells (the phloem). Stinging nettles were amongst many wild species, also including lime trees, wisteria and mulberry, that have been used in the past for harvesting textile fibres, though other more economically important sources of natural plant bast fibres today include flax and hemp. The valuable bast fibres are separated from the woodier core of the stem (the xylem tissues) through a process known as retting, either using microorganisms or chemical means. Stinging nettles have thus been used historically for many of the same purposes as linen. Despite the coarser nature of nettle bast fibres compared to cotton, they can nonetheless be grown and harvested with a far lower environmental 'footprint' than cotton due to the fact that they do not require inputs of fertilisers and pesticides — even recycling the chemical constituents of waste water — as well as being less reliant on sub-tropical or tropical climates and long transport routes to market.

Additional uses of stinging nettles include as dye-stuffs, a yellow dye extracted from the roots and yellowish-green pigments from the leaves. Given their preference for growing on phosphorus and nitrogen-rich soils, harvested nettles also make rich additions to compost or can be used when broken down as a liquid fertiliser in horticulture.

Given these diverse uses, it may horrify gardeners, who know this plant as a weed, to learn that nettles are sometimes cultivated. This occurs either by spreading seed on tilled soil in the autumn, planting pre-germinated seedlings, or vegetative propagation from sections of stolon. Stinging nettle plants can also be propagated using soil-free practices, including hydroponics using water or aeroponics using moist air or mist, reducing harvesting costs and contamination with other weed species.

HOW TO GRASP A NETTLE

Despite the warning inherent in the phrase 'grasp the nettle', there is an easy way to grasp a nettle without getting stung. This is a talent learned by many of us as youngsters, and one I still use today. The sting of a nettle, as we have seen, results from the stiff, hollow hairs penetrating the skin and breaking to inject toxins. However, if the plant is gripped firmly, especially grasped from the lower stem in an upward direction, the hairs tend to be pushed flat and the skin is not penetrated anywhere near as easily. Grasping the nettle is a skill worth propagating, both for stinging nettles and in terms of wider application to life's trials and tribulations!

14 All Creatures Great But Small

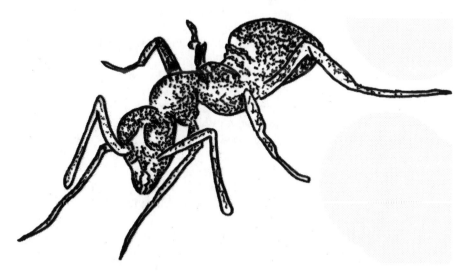

To some people, they are simply 'creepy crawlies'. For many, aside from a few of the more blousy butterflies and iridescent dragonflies, these diverse 'mini-beasts' are mainly regarded as an amorphous mix of bugs, if indeed they are not entirely dismissed. Yet, the insect world is one of huge diversity, functional importance and value to continuing human wellbeing.

In Chapter 17, *99.9% of All Known Germs*, we consider separately the smallest of small living organisms — all those microscopic 'germs' — and the many things they do. We have also given some consideration to wasps in the context of *Unappealing Creatures* (Chapter 9), and even considered the roles of some tiny insects in the context of their roles in healthy soils. But this chapter gives centre stage to insects, one of our home planet's most numerous, diverse and remarkable groups of animals.

WHAT IS AN INSECT?

So, what is an insect? Insects are a class of hexapod (six-legged) invertebrates forming the largest group within the arthropod (hinged leg) phylum. They are also the most diverse group of animals on our home planet. Best estimates suggest that there are between 6 and 10 million species of insect that potentially comprise over 90% of all animal life forms on Earth. Insects are found in nearly all environments on Earth apart from the sea, where only a small number of species occur. (The crustaceans take over as the most numerous arthropod group in marine environments.)

The insects are characterised by a chitinous exoskeleton, a three-part body (head, thorax and abdomen), three pairs of jointed legs, compound eyes and one pair of antennae. They propel themselves in a variety of ways, including walking, flying or, in the case of aquatic insects in a larval stage or else living fully aquatic lives, swimming. Insects are the only group of invertebrates to have evolved flight. Almost all insects hatch from eggs, with growth interrupted by a series of moults due to the constraints of their inelastic exoskeletons, which need to be periodically shed. Some, like the familiar butterfly life cycle, can metamorphose through widely differing forms throughout life — egg, larva, pupa (or chrysalis) and imago (adult) forms — though some skip the pupal stage and develop to adulthood through a series of nymph stages. Some insects, including the earwigs, show a degree of maternal care in guarding their eggs and young.

Insects can also communicate with each other. Pond skaters exhibit some social structure, interacting by sensing vibrations in the surface film of the ponds and rivers they inhabit. Male moths are attracted chemically through the release pheromones (hormonal substances released external to the body) by females of their species. Crickets, cicadas and some other insects communicate with sounds. Lampyrid beetles — soft-bodied beetles known as fireflies or lightning bugs including Europe's common glow worm (*Lampyris noctiluca*) — communicate by emitting light.

The insects range in size from a tiny fairyfly, *Dicopomorpha echmepterygis*, that is a parasitoid (has larvae that kill their host but with a free-living adult phase) living on the eggs of other insects, right up to the five species of goliath beetle (*Goliathus* species) the males of which range from 60 to 110 millimetres (2.4–4.3 inches) long. But even these modern-day monsters are puny compared to some fossilized insects from the Palaeozoic era, amongst them dragonfly-like *Meganeura* with wingspans of 55–70 centimetres (22–28 inches). The most diverse insect groups appear to have co-evolved with flowering plants, developing mutually advantageous relationships that include playing key roles in plant pollination.

LOATHE THEM OR LOVE THEM

In common with other *Unappealing Creatures*, including the slugs, wasps and woodlice that we met earlier in this book, people have tended to regard certain types of insects purely as pests to be controlled using insecticides and other techniques. And it is true that some insects cause damage to crops by feeding on sap, leaves, fruits or wood, whereas other species are parasitic or, as in the case of mosquitoes, can be a vector for the microbial agents of livestock and human diseases such as malaria, dengue fever, West Nile virus and Zika virus.

However, the huge diversity of insects perform a range of functions in the environment that we largely overlook, though many or most of them are of great if unappreciated importance. As some examples, a variety of flies consume carrion (dead animal matter) whilst others are important pollinators crucial to the life cycles of many flowering plant species, including of significant crops used by humans. Other insects, including those pesky wasps, amongst a wide range of groups, are predators of other organisms that might otherwise become pests. Silkworms produce silk, honey bees produce honey and some insects are consumed as human food in 80% of countries throughout the world.

For many people, insects — gaudy butterflies, elegant leaf insects, laborious ants, the hum of busy bees, musical crickets, the crazy dance on pond surfaces of the whirlygig beetle, and many others — have entrancing beauty and/or fascinating life habits. Other insects divide public opinion whilst most are entirely overlooked. All, however, serve some purpose or other on this planet as tightly co-evolved elements in the functioning of ecosystems. We will look at some of these benefits in the following sections of this chapter, as well as considering the many ways in which human activities also impact insect biodiversity to our considerable potential detriment. But, whether we understand or like them or not, it would be foolhardy to continue on our current development trajectory that is driving them to extinction.

So why should we care about these amazing creatures?

INSECTS MAKE THE WORLD GO AROUND

Well, for starters, many species of bird, bat, reptile, amphibian, small mammal and fish would simply die out, as they would have nothing to eat were insects to disappear. Not only do insects make up the vast bulk of known species on this planet but, as integrally co-evolved elements of the ecosystems in which they occur, they are the principal food sources of many other animals. And, additionally to supporting those animals that eat them directly, insects play important roles connecting all terrestrial and freshwater food webs. Insects connect cycles of energy, nutrients and other chemicals in nature's complex ecological networks, playing key roles in many other ecosystem functions.

But it is not just animals that owe their survival to the insects. An estimated 87% of all plant species — pretty much all plants species excluding grasses and conifers — rely on animals for pollination, and most of this pollination service is delivered by insects.[1] Pollination by insects, also known as 'entomophily', often relies on flowers that are conspicuous to insects including by scents, food rewards including both pollen and nectar, bright colours and/or elaborate marks that act as guides for landing patterns. Some of these visual signals are visible to us humans — visit any florist or summer garden for obvious evidence of that — but other visual clues are at light wavelengths beyond the range of our senses. We have all probably seen the extending mouthparts of butterflies and bees adapted to suck out these nourishing treats from flowers, many insects specifically co-evolved with specific plants, or types of plant, and correspondingly crucial to the successful pollination of their floral hosts.

Early terrestrial plants appear to have been largely dependent on wind pollination, releasing pollen into surrounding air currents with the minute chance of grains being carried to and landing on receptive female plant parts. However, the angiosperms (flowering plants) appear to have evolved a new pollination strategy at some time between 125 and 115 million years ago in the Early Cretaceous period. By working synergistically and co-beneficially with insects, flowering plants

---

[1] Ollerton, J., Winfree, R. and Tarrant, S. (2011). How many flowering plants are pollinated by animals? *Oikos*, 120, pp. 321–326.

achieved huge competitive advantage by the targeting of pollen, averting the need to produce and liberate vast quantities to the vagaries of the wind. As we have seen, entomophilous plant species have frequently evolved a wide array of mechanisms to make themselves appealing often to specific insects through a range of visual, scent and other clues. Some of these scents are sweet and advertise food — we know this from the fragrance of many blossoms — whereas others mimic insect pheromones, and still more emit the odour of carrion to attract flies (a trait known as sapro-myophily). Beetles, bees, butterflies, moths, a diversity of types of flies and midges, wasps and some ants are all commonplace pollinators. In some plants, such as the European cuckoo pint (*Arum maculatum*), also known as 'lords and ladies', flies attracted to the scent — in this case of a rotting carcass — are trapped enabling them to become coated in pollen, before erectile hairs inside the flower relax letting the fly out again to seek other cuckoo pint flowers to which they transfer pollen. Other insect-flower relationships are far more specialised through co-evolution, such as the flowers of the bee orchid (*Ophrys apifera*) that mimic bees both in visual appearance — the flower's velvety lip looks like a female bee — and also scent, attracting male bees that attempt to mate transferring pollen in the process.

All of these specialised interactions between insects and other animals and plants indicate the depth of co-evolution and importance of this group of often neglected small animals in maintaining the structure, functioning and resilience of the eco-systems of Planet Earth.

FOOD FOR FREE

We also rely on insects for the food that we, perhaps unthinkingly, put on our plates every day. Approximately three-quarters of all crop types grown by humans require pollination by insects. Take away the insects, or allow their populations to decline, and we face a serious threat of food insecurity. Of course, the humanitarian disaster of food insufficiency is beyond economic measure but, as a 'free' service from nature, the global value of insect pollination has been estimated at between $235 billion and $577 billion per year based on global crop yields of 60 pollination dependent or profiting crops. The same study also found that, from 2009, increases in producer prices for pollination-dependent crops may be early warnings of the consequences of declining pollinator populations. Financial aspects aside, we simply could not feed the global human population without pollinators.

In the United States, large agricultural concerns hire bee hives on large flatbed trailers positioned in croplands to compensate for the loss of natural pollination functions. In parts of China, people are hired manually to transfer pollen between plants where pollinating insects have been decimated. From Australia to Europe and beyond, the hiring of smaller-scale bee hives is a common solution for increasing pollination, often under written pollination agreements specifying the responsi-bilities of both parties including what happens to the hives once they are in the crop. All this, of course, highlights the importance and considerable value of these often neglected pollinating insects, indicating also the detrimental effects of their decline.

On Monday 14th May 2018, Germany's Penny Market discount supermarket store in Hannover used its corporate influence to surprise its substantial customer base by removing products pollinated by bees, substantially emptying its shelves.[2] People coming to shop, with no forewarning, found that apples, zucchini, baked goods, chocolate, sweets coated with beeswax, some marinated meats and chamomile-scented toilet paper were amongst many products removed from the shelves. Penny Market assessed that in the region of 60% of the 2,500 products it was selling were directly or indirectly dependant on bee pollination. The purpose of the company's action was to draw public attention to, and stimulate concern about, the significant implications of the drastic decline in bee populations over recent decades, a Penny Markets spokesman reportedly saying *'We were hoping for a eureka moment'*. The supermarket's campaign preceded the United Nations first World Bee Day on 20th May 2018.

Further contributions from insects to food production include the roles of many insect groups — ladybirds, hoverflies, ground beetles, lacewings, wasps, and numerous more — as biocontrol agents. Through predation on potential pest insects and other organisms, or else acting as parasites upon them, these generally unsung insect heroes often play major roles in successful crop production.

Many types of insect, many of them tiny such as springtails and silverfish, break down leaves, animal corpses and other organic matter on or in the soil. A range of wood boring beetles and wasps also help recycle nutrients in decaying timber. Animal dung is integrated into soils by the activities of flies, beetles and countless other small life, drawn into the soil by ants and other burrowing insects, the actions of which also help increase soil permeability, tilth and aeration. These insects also help in the dispersal of seeds.

The global decline in insect diversity and numbers is a grave cause for concern for many reasons, amongst them implications for food security. Countervailing these pressures, mainly driven by habitat loss and the incautious and widespread use of pesticides in society, there is growing recognition of the tangible value of integrating wild strips — beetle banks, buffer strips along field boundaries, etc. — as well as retaining hedgerows in farmed land as a reservoir for pollinating and predatory insects and other wildlife. This can bring real value to farmed land, nature doing what nature does best and averting applications of pesticides that can only hasten the decline of insect populations and the many services they provide for free.

PUTTING INSECTS TO WORK

Other insects are put directly into productive uses by people.

Apiculture, or the practice of keeping any of a range of bee species, has a very long history. Whilst there are depictions of people collecting honey from wild bees dating back an estimated 10,000 years, archaeological evidence dates beekeeping in pottery vessels from 9,000 years ago in North Africa. Depictions of domesticated bees and the use of smoke to pacify the hives also feature in Egyptian art from around 4,500 years ago, and honey stored in jars has been found in the tombs of

---

[2] The Local. (2019). Bee-n and gone: Hanover supermarket warns customers of bee-less world. *The Local*, 15 May 2018. (https://www.thelocal.de/20180515/hanover-shop-empties-shelves-of-bee-pollinated-products, accessed 26 May 2020.)

pharaohs including that of Tutankhamun (died 1324 BCE). The advent of construction of hives with movable combs dates back to the 18th century in Europe,
enabling the harvesting of honey without destroying the colony. Honey has served
as a prestigious and nutritious human food source for millennia. It was also used as
a sugar source in the production of mead wine, most strongly associated with
mediaeval Europe, Africa and Asia where it has played a role in some mythology.
But the history of honey-based mead wine may be far longer, as pottery vessels
dating from 7000 BCE discovered in northern China have shown chemical sig-
natures consistent with the presence of honey, rice and organic compounds associated with fermentation.

Silk is another insect product with high economic and cultural significance. Silk
is a natural protein fibre produced by diverse groups of insects as well as spiders.
However, the vast majority of silk that is woven into textiles is derived from the
cocoons of a select number of insect larvae, the best known of which is the mulberry silkworm (*Bombyx mori*). Silkworm larvae are reared in captivity, a practice
known as sericulture generally entailing feeding them mulberry leaves on trays, and
are harvested as they spin a cocoon of silk in which to pupate. The pupae are killed
either by being dipping in boiling water before the adult moth emerges, or by
piercing them with a needle. These practices have led animal rights campaigners to
protest against the practice and trade. However, these treatments enhance the ability
of sericulturalists to unravel the whole cocoon as a single continuous thread,
creating a much stronger cloth when woven. Development of silk fabrics occurred
first in ancient China, the silk protein fibroin found in soil samples from tombs at a
Neolithic site in Henan dating back around 8,500 years. The oldest known surviving
example of silk fabric dates from around 3630 BCE, also from Henan. The luxurious
texture and lustre of silk meant that it became an opulent fabric, and consequently
was in high demand becoming a staple product in pre-industrial international trade.

Spreading from China despite attempts by Chinese emperors to keep the
knowledge of sericulture secret, silk production and trade spread as far as Korea,
the Indian subcontinent, the Middle East, Europe and North Africa. India is now
the second-largest producer of silk after China, and is also the world's largest
consumer of silk used in a range of traditions including the wearing of silk
sarees for marriages and other auspicious ceremonies. During World War II,
supplies of silk used in the UK for making parachutes were secured from the
Middle East. The high strength of silk means that it has been put to many
other uses, ranging from adding attractive lustre to furniture and curtains, in industrial applications such as bicycle tyres and artillery gunpowder bags, and as
medical sutures.

Silk may in fact have been one of the driving forces of the world's first wave of
globalisation, giving its name to the 'Silk Roads' establishing trade routes between
western Eurasia and the Far East from the 1st century BCE to the 18th century.[3]

---

[3] Vanham, P. (2019). *A Brief History of Globalization*. World Economic Forum (WEF). [Online.]
(https://www.weforum.org/agenda/2019/01/how-globalization-4-0-fits-into-the-history-of-
globalisation/, accessed 26 May 2020.)

This pre-industrial trade also included spices and other commodities, the production of which also entailed the activities of insects. Transfer of learning accompanied trade and traders, another indirect contribution to the evolution of civilisation supported by this groups of insects.

INSECT INSPIRATION

Architects have sought inspiration from the actions of insects, ranging from the strong cellular structures within the papery nests of wasps to the natural air conditioning of towers built by colonies of termites. Insects and their parts have featured in jewellery throughout history, and as an inspiration to man-made versions. *The Wasps*, incidental music written by British composer Ralph Vaughan Williams in 1909, the *Madam Butterfly* opera written by Giacomo Puccini premiering in 1904 and Nicolai Rimsky-Korsakov's 1899 *The Flight of the Bumblebee* are three better-known pieces of classical music inspired by insects and their habits, and there are many more insect-inspired contemporary works to enjoy.

Insects have also, perhaps unsurprisingly, been imbued with spiritual meanings, both negative and positive. The 'plague of locusts' of the Bible is one of the former, ancient Hebrews also seeing flies as the manifestation of evil with Beelzebub, the devil incarnate, known as *Lord of the Flies*. Conversely, scarab beetles were seen as of spiritual significance by Ancient Egyptians as their habit of rolling balls of dung were considered a manifestation of the transit of the sun across the sky each day, rolled by a giant celestial dung beetle. Moths and butterflies have been seen as evocative of the spirit and of joy from Ancient Greece to African and in countless other traditions. Other metamorphosing insects have been seen as emblematic of resurrection, for example, as cicadas are to Buddhists.

And, of course, there is branch of science known as lepidopterology: the study of butterflies and moths. Whilst early practitioners, particularly in the Victorian era, tended to collect, kill and preserve specimens, sometimes in vast numbers, this practice is now thankfully less common, though remains valid for some scientific purposes. Butterfly photography is a more fulfilling practice, though some insects are truly evasive, as of course are night-flying moths and a range of other nocturnal, tiny or otherwise elusive mini-beasts. 'Mini-beasts' is a term that entered the primary school curriculum in the United Kingdom, a welcome acquaintance for children with a range of small animals with which they share their lives.

It is hard to quantify the overall importance of all the things that insects do, as we simply do not know what many insects do within ecosystems. Furthermore, something like 80% of all of the millions of insect species on Earth remain unnamed by science. Given the huge complexity of natural ecosystems, and the multiple pathways and interactions within them, it would be ill-judged to suggest that any insect is of no importance, be that for pollination, decomposition, pest control, nutrient cycling, artistic inspiration, spiritual meaning, food, or any of a host of other purposes both known and unknown.

ADDRESSING THE DECLINE IN INSECT POPULATIONS

The decline of insect populations has been described as 'the unnoticed apocalypse'.

Human activities have reduced the abundance of wildlife on Earth dramatically, driving once-common species to scarcity and some less-common organisms to extinction. The total population of the world's wild vertebrates (fish, amphibians, reptiles, mammals and birds) was estimated to have fallen by 60% between the years 1970 and 2014.[4] Amazingly, another study calculated that wild mammals now only account for 4% of global mammalian biomass, humans comprising 36% and our livestock a staggering 60%. In all, 70% of global bird biomass is now accounted for by domestic poultry.[5] These paces of decline of wild species, and the overwhelming dominance of humanity on this planet, are massive and far from unlikely to avoid presaging significant problems. However, bear in mind that these studies address just the bigger creatures with which we share this world. The substantial majority of known species are invertebrates, many of which, at least in habitats other than the sea, are accounted for by insects that we know to be functionally important if still largely unexplored. The problems of wildlife decline and the implications for humanity may therefore be vastly bigger than that indicated by data on larger species. A number of scientific reports describing the rapid decline of insects right across the world, in some localities in catastrophic collapse, should give us all cause for grave concern. And this, bear in mind, amongst a group of organisms that are poorly studied; the real situation may be far worse. We appear to be in the midst of the largest extinction event on Earth since the late Permian (a geological epoch 250 million years ago).

The situation, though serious, is not beyond salvation. Stopping the incautious use of pesticides in urban parkland and gardens, and in agriculture and forestry, would make a massive difference. Reversing our former habit of converting urban and rural habitats into insect-unfriendly deserts can also make a substantial difference as habitat loss is another major factor in insect decline. We can also do a great deal more to manage habitats to encourage insects, for example, for their beneficial uses in farmland but also along verges, railway routes and riverbanks, school playgrounds and sports fields. We could do more to link up areas important for all types of wildlife, and which may be 'hotspots' for insect populations, such that they are able to move through our current wildlife-unfriendly landscapes.

MULTUM IN PARVO

The Latin phrase 'multum in parvo' literally means 'much in little'. This is an appropriate way to think of the much-neglected but hugely important group of all creatures great but small, many known as the insects. They may be small, but their impact on the functioning of our home planet is huge, and most certainly deserving of our great respect and greater care.

---

[4] WWF (2018). *Living Planet Report — 2018: Aiming Higher*. Grooten, M. and Almond, R.E.A. (Eds). WWF: Gland, Switzerland.

[5] Bar-On, Y.M., Phillips, R. and Milo, R. (2018). The biomass distribution on Earth. *PNAS*, 115, pp. 6506–6511.

15 Feel the Noise

'In space, no one can hear you scream' was the tagline in the 1979 space horror movie *Alien*, directed by Ridley Scott. The movie was a blockbuster, spawning three sequels and arguably also seeding a genre. However, what is of interest here is that the tagline is based on an environmental fact: without an environment to transmit vibrations, there can be no sound.

Sound is all around us, a generally overlooked 'mood music' of the day from the hum of the computer's cooling systems or the bees, to the music of birdsong or human-made instruments, the bark of a fox or human speech, or the intrusion of traffic noise or forewarning of rising storm winds. Sound is so pervasive that we probably don't stop often enough to wonder what it is, and what it means. We also probably don't often pause to equate it as having an ecology, or to recognise the diverse ways that it affects us in both positive and negative ways.

SOUND AND NOISE

In rather stark physical terms, sound is a vibration that propagates as an acoustic wave through a transmission medium, be that medium a gas — as in the case of air — or a liquid or solid. We turn vibrations into what we perceive as sound by funnelling them with our outer ears to the tympanic membrane (or eardrum), through three linked small bones in the middle ear, and into nerve cells in the cochlea of the inner ear that turn them into electrical signals. These electrical signals are interpreted by the auditory cortex (part of the brain's temporal lobe in humans and many other vertebrates) into what we perceive as sound.

For humans, the spectrum of audible vibrations is between roughly 20 Hertz (beats per second) and 20,000 Hertz (20 kHz), though our sensitivity to higher frequencies reduces as we age. Sound waves above 20 kHz are known as ultrasound as they are not audible to humans, whereas sound waves below 20 Hz are known as infrasound and are also inaudible to us though we may register them as physical vibrations. Different animal species have varying hearing ranges adapted to their life style. Some species of bats, for example, can hear up to frequencies of 200 kHz, though do not hear very well below 10 kHz. Conversely, whales generally hear from a subsonic 30 Hz up to about 8,000 Hz (8 kHz).

The term 'sound' is value neutral. Some of it is pleasing and soothing or inspiring, for example, the mellifluous tones of wild birds or the music we choose. Some is quite the reverse — a noisy neighbour, a low-flying jet plane, or a backfiring car — and this we label as 'noise'. 'Noise' is defined broadly by acousticians (experts in the branch of physics concerned with the properties of sound) simply as 'unwanted sound'.

Neither of these types of sound, the welcome and the intrusive, have thresholds. The first subtle twittering of the dawn chorus may rouse us from deep slumber and the near-deafening roar of a waterfall can be inspiring and uplifting. Conversely, the title of Rachel Carson's famous 1963 book *Silent Spring*, warning of the dangers of the bioaccumulation of persistent pesticides, was impactful as an auditory metaphor: a spring robbed of familiar and uplifting birdsong by poisoning at the hands of humanity would be awful. Likewise, a quiet but persistently annoying dripping tap may be as disturbing as a pneumatic drill.

THE ECOLOGY OF SOUNDS

We and other species have a diversity of senses, some species having far greater sensitivities to different environmental stimuli than others. Sound has strengths and weaknesses in terms of other stimuli. Unlike odour, sound is unidirectional, instantaneous leaving no trace and moves rapidly over longer distances.

It is funny how different sounds can affect different species rather differently. I have already mentioned how inspiring — thrilling even — the dawn chorus is when it filters through windows and consciousness on spring dawns. Starting in around 5:45 am in the early part of April in the UK (06:45 central European time), and progressively earlier as daylength extends, the concerto often starts with the mellifluous voice of a blackbird, progressively augmented by twittering and fluting from robins and various other small brown choristers, the choir swelling progressively as various tits and other invisible vocalists join the throng. Later in the cycle, an increasingly scarce cuckoo may echo from the cover of a distant wood. Often, the loudest amongst them is the disproportionately massive vocalisation of the tiniest of wrens. From sporadic fluting, the overture builds, swelling over long minutes to evolve into a central movement of full song. Then, progressively, the song cycle wanes after anything between a half-hour and a full hour, with often a momentary pause before the coarse crackle of rooks and the cooing of wood pigeons signal a segue into the sounds of full daytime.

As the daylight strengthens, other sounds of full daytime take their place, including the flapping squabble of wood pigeons on the power line running in front of the house. The noises of busy humanity also increasingly intrude, as the spell of nature in largely uninterrupted finery is broken.

However, from the perspective of the birds themselves, the magical dawn chorus is little more than a mass clarion cry of sex and violence! Why would a potential prey animal announce itself so stridently to the wider world, often making itself even more conspicuous by finding a perch on a tree top or high branch from which to project its voice, if not for compelling reasons of survival? Doing so in the half-light when most sight-dependent predators such as sparrow hawks are at a disadvantage is a cunning strategy. However, it is still one entailing risk. Birdsongs, for all their beauty, are a necessity. In the main, they are an announcement staking a territorial claim on the new day as well as a call to potential mates at the outset of the breeding season.

The clarion cry of the kingfisher — a loud 'peep' as it arrows up or down the river — is a warning to potential intruders of literally murderous intent to defend its territory. So too the growl of a tiger, the roar of a lion and the bark of a stag, these also an invitation to potential mates. The rattlesnake does not rattle other than as a warning, and the blackbird's alarm call tells others of its species that there is danger around.

The directional and high-speed nature of sound also means that it is used by various species for navigation. It is well known that bats use echolocation to navigate their environments, including in complete darkness. In fact, more than half of the approximately 900 known species of bats rely on echolocation to detect obstacles in flight, to find their way into roosts and to forage for food. Echolocation in essence allows the bat to 'see' with sound through active use of sonar (Sound Navigation And Ranging). They achieve this by emitting auditory signals, generally through the larynx but some 'clicking' with their tongues, sensing reflected sound waves to detect physical objects. The frequencies of these sounds can range, depending on bat species, from 20 Hz to as high as 200 kHz, way beyond those that humans can hear. The discovery of this ability has a fascinating history, prior to realisation that sounds extended beyond human sensitivity. However, bats are just one group amongst a few other mammals that use sound to navigate, including some shrews and tenrecs (Tenrecidae, a family of mammals unique to Madagascar). Some nocturnal birds also echolocate, including the nocturnal oilbird and some swiftlets.

Whales, porpoises and dolphins also echolocate, doing so in water rather than air. Water has certain advantages over air in terms of sound transmission due to its greater density, sound travelling about four-and-a-half times faster underwater. Some whale song is detectable over a range of thousands of kilometres. The general principles of sonar location apply underwater, though sound frequencies are generally far lower than those used by bats owing to the physical properties of fresh and saline water.

At lower frequencies too, fish use pressure waves that are generally at lower frequencies than those we refer to as sound, though the senses we distinguish as feeling and sound tend to overlap for fish. Immersed in the dense medium of water, various groups of fishes have heightened sensitivities to acoustic and other vibration signals, detecting objects around them by pressure waves. The swim bladder in some groups of fishes, an air-filled organ modifying buoyancy, can detect and amplify sounds in the surrounding watery medium. Most groups of fishes have an elaborate acoustico-lateralis system, typically taking the form of a lateral line of pits along all or part of the body and sometimes the head, containing epidermal sensory neuromast cells. Experimentally blinded minnows and some other fishes are still able to navigate their environments, and there are numerous cave-dwelling fish species around the world that live, navigate and feed in total darkness. Some amphibians, such as frogs, also have lateral line organs, though their neural connections disappear during metamorphosis of tadpoles into adults, that no longer need to feed underwater.

Other low-frequency sound is detectible by a range of animals. Earthworms, for example, detect the patter of rain on the soil surface as a signal for them to emerge at the surface to seek out organic matter on which to feed and potentially to mate with other worms in adjacent burrows when not at risk of dehydration. This behaviour is exploited by blackbirds, some gulls and other bird species, which can be observed running or stamping on the ground to mimic rainfall, picking off emerging worms.

At even lower sound frequencies still, the deathwatch beetle (*Xestobium rufovillosum*), a woodboring species of beetle that tends to infest structural timbers in old buildings, attracts mates by tapping on the timber. The ticking sound that can sometimes be heard in the rafters of old buildings on summer nights is the basis of the common name of the beetle, long associated as a harbinger of death as it is most audible on quiet nights in the rafters of old houses, and consequently during silent bedside vigils for the dying.

HOW NOISE AFFECTS WILDLIFE

Noise, in this case the pervasive and invasive sounds produced by human activities and particularly those resulting from mechanisation, can be disturbing not merely to us humans but to wildlife too.

During the 2020 lockdown in India in response to the Covid-19 pandemic, friends of mine in the major cities of Mumbai, Delhi and Jaipur remarked not only about the unprecedented cleanliness and clarity of the air and of rivers, but also that birds had returned to the city. Noise and general bustle were significant factors formerly driving them out. I was also told that Gangetic river dolphins were sighted far closer to cities than had been known in many decades, though how much of this was due to substantially improved water clarity and therefore visibility as opposed to a real spread of dolphins is uncertain. However, as echolocating animals, underwater cacophony from boat traffic and activities on the surrounding land can hardly be attractants. In the marine environment, noise from ships and other intrusive human activities is known to be harmful to whales and dolphins through interference with echolocation, including strong implications that the use of sonar by the military has been a driving factor behind some mass whale stranding events. Wider ecological interferences are all but inevitable as many animals use sound for reasons as diverse as navigation, locating food, attracting mates and avoiding predators. For example, some studies on the ecological impacts of sound have found that noise pollution can accelerate the heartbeats of caterpillars and reduce brood size in some birds. There is highly likely to be a great deal more that we do not know about the diffuse impacts of noise on the natural world.

SOUND AND HUMAN WELLBEING

Potential impacts of noise pollution on wildlife are poorly understood, but the same is true for humans. Back in the early 2000s, the UK Environment Secretary of the time, Michael Meacher MP, described noise as the 'Cinderella pollutant'. Little has changed over the intervening decades. However, its implications may be severe.

The World Health Organisation has identified the burden of disease from environmental noise as the second highest after air pollution. Addressing this form of pollutant is complex as noise is a complex subject: the primary immediate effect is annoyance, which is a subjective experience. Furthermore, noise does not leave lasting traces and, often, comes from multiple everyday sources and other origins that may be hard to identify. Although noise can, as we say, 'drive us to distraction', people also habituate to noise — or in other words 'get used to it' — over time. Yet, an increasing body of scientific studies has found that long-term exposure to moderate noise levels common in towns and cities can increase levels of stress and rises in blood pressure whether or not sufferers are consciously aware of this backdrop of intrusive sounds and its effects upon them. These factors can be contributory to increased incidence of cardiac illness and other adverse, secondary effects.

Measures to control unwanted noise are not new. The Ancient Greeks and Romans implemented specific civic ordinances designed to reduce annoyance due to noise. A 'Cinderella pollutant' indeed as, though the Cinderella story common to English speakers can be traced back to the French story 'Cendrillon' published in 1697 by Charles Perrault, Chinese and Greek versions of the classic tale go back to the 9th century CE and 6th century BCE, respectively.

The other side of the picture is that the rhythmic swish of waves on a beach can sooth, and playing whale song is recommended to pacify unborn children in the womb. The patter of a shower on a canopy of leaves, the swish of the leaves of aspen trees in a summer breeze, and the dawn chorus can exhilarate and refresh. Edward O Wilson famously defined the term 'Biophilia' — the innate tendency of humans to seek connections with nature and other forms of lifetime — and the corollary that alienation from nature could cause stress and distress.[1] A natural

---

[1] Wilson, E.O. (1990). *Biophilia (New Edition)*. Harvard University Press.

affinity born of our evolutionary past for loving a spectrum of natural sounds should not be surprising, nor that natural sounds have been found to decrease the human body's flight-or-fight response. Natural sounds as well as peace and quiet are therefore potentially healing, relaxing and de-stressing. So too many of the sounds that we create.

World history is full of references to 'soul music'; not just the soul music of African American origins appearing in the United States from the 1950s and 1960s, but 'music for the soul' as a metaphor for peaceful and uplifting music of any genre. So too 'music of the spheres' as a metaphor for harmonious and edifying experiences and concepts. Before the 'talkies', piano and other music was played live to amplify the emotional content of silent films, and modern film music is a central part of the sensory experience. Heaven, we are told, also has its harp playing choirs of angels to soothe the soul, amplifying the centrality of sound as part of the human experience. We also find healing in tranquillity, conflating 'peace and quiet' albeit that the word 'peace' highlights the sense of freedom from disturbance of the quietness of desirable sounds.

SOUNDING OFF

Sound connects us, to each other and to the world around us. A 'silent spring' would be a tragedy, in more ways than one. In that delicious half-slumbering state on first waking, I am happy to allow my scientific mind a little rest and to float with the poets with the waxing and waning of the dawn symphony. From Chaucer to Bernard Shaw, poets have celebrated the dawn chorus, birdsong inspiring music in many forms from Vaughan Williams to Beethoven, Vivaldi and Benjamin Britten.

There is, in fact, an International Dawn Chorus Day set on the first Sunday of May, albeit that the preceding month is often the time of richest tunefulness. Framed as a worldwide celebration of nature's greatest symphony, International Dawn Chorus Day encourages people across the world to rise early to experience the magnificence of the dawn soundscape. Many do so, though very many more do not, or at least do not intentionally, as the dawn chorus by that date starts closer to 4:00 in the morning in the UK. However, in reality, the 'International' tag is mainly a British invention as, down in the southern hemisphere, autumn is already progressing at pace towards winter.

Whatever its biological functions and the tags that humans put upon it, the dawn chorus is a thing of beauty and wonder, a free gift from the natural world. It is a balm for the soul, lightning whatever concerns may otherwise clamour for our attention. To wake with the birds is a wonderful thing.

16 No Place Like Home

At some indeterminate time in history, a small settlement gathered around a place on the river that could be crossed in summer weather. The river gave freely of its water for drinking, bathing and stock watering. Its fertile floodplains supported crops and grazing, and the land and waterscape dealt with wastes of various types as well as supplying willow, celandines, dandelions, meadowsweet, sloes and all manner of other plants of medicinal, nutritious and ornamental value.

A COMMUNITY FORMS

The land above the break of slope was flat and dry enough for the building of homes, so a community developed supported by the bounty of the river, the floodplain and the surrounding woodland which provided for building and fuel needs as well as breaking the power of storms. The hills around yielded yellow Cotswold stone for building and clay for brick-making. Fish and fowl from the wetlands and hay and other fibre from the drier lands added to the wealth of natural riches.

The auspicious nature of the river crossing that saw frequent travellers and traders gave the settlement soul and sustenance, and perhaps even some spiritual significance leading to the founding of an ancient church and probably other religious settlements from times before that which were subsequently redeveloped in the Christian era. It also gave the place a name. The village of Great Somerford in North Wiltshire, in the west country of England, is that summer ford across the river, and the place I have called home for well over a quarter of a century.

Clearly, I was not here to see all of this history! But the name itself — originally Somerford Magna — and other heritage and local history renders my conjuring a matter of more substance than wild speculation alone.

THE POWERS OF ECOSYSTEMS

My reason for this telling of tales of yore is that we overlook the importance and power of ecosystems and their services in the everyday places we inhabit to an alarming extent. This is a matter of far more than wishful thinking that we should think 'greener', or with misplaced nostalgia. It is because, if we ignore it, we are highly likely to degrade the fundamental natural wealth supporting our wellbeing along with the interests of all who share it, including those yet to come, in the decisions that we make in the here and now. However well-intentioned those decisions may be, if they ignore the significance and vitality of the natural resources that support us all, the outcomes, particularly the unforeseen outcomes, are likely to be far from beneficial.

In the modern Great Somerford, water for domestic, agricultural and light industrial use is no longer drawn from the river but is piped from aquifers tens of miles away, though some natural watering of farmland and of livestock remains important. Likewise, waste water is treated electromechanically before being discharged to the river above the main bridge connecting Little Somerford and Great Somerford. The food consumed in the village is by vast majority now procured not by harvesting from local fields and hedgerows but accessed using our oil-fuelled chariots driven to supermarkets miles away, themselves supplied from across the globe by carbon-intense supply chains. Construction materials for modern housing too have supply chains reaching way beyond the gates of the builders' merchants in adjacent towns. The medicines used by today's village people may be produced industrially by pharmaceutical giants, not drawn with traditional wisdom from local flora and fauna, though these modern drugs are often analogues of the natural pharmacopeia. This genetic and chemical resource still holds many more as yet unexplored or unexploited resources of potential value in future livestock breeding, crop and medical applications.

Yet, however apparently far removed, nature is always there supplying and regenerating the raw materials, serving as a source of energy, cleaning up the messes, draining the floodwater and storing moisture to tide us through the drier months. The communities of the Somerfords remain characterised by their local river and the landscape it has sculpted, enjoying the recreational and scenic gifts it bestows. Its soils grow our plants at home and in the allotment, and the communities formed around farming, fishing, gardening, allotmenteering, wildlife and other natural focal interests bind us together.

We also remain vulnerable to extremes of drought, flood and storm, all the more so when development encroaches onto floodplains. This vulnerability is increased both locally and in communities affected downstream receiving the magnified impacts of flood surges generated by our use and abuse of natural, functional floodplains, buffering woodlands, vegetative cover averting soil erosion and other of nature's regulating services. The green spaces in our village are of value for their character and amenity, not to mention the hydrology and wider ecology of the place.

IN A NAME

Some communities have entirely expunged the natural wealth of rivers upon which they were founded. In London, for example, the Kye Burn that gave Kilburn its name, the Strand that is now a street rather than a shoreline, and Bayards Watering Hole (today best known by its contracted name of Bayeswater) all come to mind as examples repeated the length and breadth of the British Isles and the developed world of rivers once vital to human settlement and development yet now expunged by it. How much of nature's supporting foundations can we afford to lose before the edifice of myopic society becomes too top-heavy, and how much compensatory investment in longer, more energy-intensive and internationally exploitative supply chains is tolerable, whether ecologically, socially or economically?

It is important that we value the commonplace in all the common places, the flow of cool water in our rivers and the life-giving characteristics of the places we inhabit and perhaps take too much for granted, or perhaps have already expunged from value and memory but for a few half memories frozen in place-names.

It is for this reason that it is vital increasingly to celebrate more of the commonplace, and the many ways in which nature supports our needs yet that appear to be far too easily forgotten. It is not merely informative and insightful to champion the ecology of everyday things, it is also important as, if it is not unearthed and cherished, it may be gone forever along with its capacity to bear us into a more secure, just and fulfilling future.

17 99.9% of All Known Germs

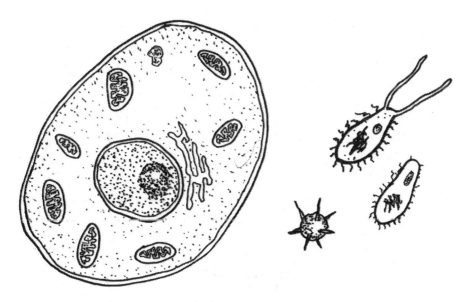

Whichever way you look at it, 'germs' have a terrible reputation.

In common parlance, a germ is generally perceived to be a microbe causing disease. They are the villainously depicted targets of many bleach and other cleaning product advertisements. Numerous advertising pronouncements promise that a miracle product will kill 99.9% of them. Germs, we see on the small screen, are lurking there waiting to attack us when we least expect it. Nasty things, like diminutive muggers lurking in dark shadows within our sinks and bathrooms.

We also hear about 'germ warfare', a synonym for the more technical term 'biological warfare'. This nasty branch of warfare entails deploying infectious microbial agents or biological toxins in the seemingly unquenchable paranoia of governments that leads them to divert substantial proportions of public funds towards increasingly ingenious means to kill enemies, be their perceived or real. These microbes — mainly various types of bacteria, virus and fungi but also including some insects — are weaponised as 'bioweapons' or 'bio-agents' intended to incapacitate or kill people, or to destroy animals or plants. All rather unpleasant stuff, and rightly the subject of international law under the Biological Weapons Convention (in force from 1975) with biological toxins also covered under the Chemical Weapons Convention (from 1997). These two Conventions augment the 1925 Geneva Protocol (the 'The Protocol for the Prohibition of the Use in War of Asphyxiating, Poisonous or other Gases, and of Bacteriological Methods of Warfare'). But these associations only serve to reinforce the bad reputation of the humble 'germ' in the public psyche.

The reality, however, could not be more different; without all these 'germs', life would be impossible for us humans and, indeed, for all life on Planet Earth.

THE ROLE OF 'GERMS' IN THE ECOSYSTEMS UPON WHICH WE RELY

For all our large and expanding population, we humans are generally arrogant in regard to our place on this planet.

Take as just one example springtails, comprising around 6,000 species of small insect-like arthropods also known as 'Collembola'. Springtails are massive compared to the microscopic 'germs' that are the subject of this chapter, ranging in length from just a quarter of a millimetre up to a whopping 1 centimetre. Estimates of their ubiquity on global landscapes suggest there are around 10,000 to 200,000 of them in every square metre of soil in most habitats on Earth. The wider group of insects too are profuse, the world's 14,000 or so species of ant comprising the most numerous group of animals on Earth, also present in virtually every millimetre of the Earth's terrestrial surface. For all the numbers of this fauna, the global terrestrial biomass of plants is around 1,000 times greater than that of all animals combined. But, again, human arrogance comes into play if it blinds us to anything that we cannot see with our own eyes.

Estimates of the global biomass of bacteria are subject to wide variability, yet may be as much as the total biomass of plants and animals combined. Estimates of fungal biomass suggest that it may be as much as a quarter of total global biomass. And that is before we start looking at other 'germs': the archaea, ciliates, flagellates, protozoa and diverse other groups of microbial organisms with which we share our world, yet with which we are barely familiar.

We may have been taught about cycles in nature in terms of photosynthesis by trees and grasses, and respiration in grazing and predatory animals. These players combine to generate cycles of carbon, water, nutrients, energy and other essential resources. Yet, in reality, the visible world is a mere bit-part player in the great biogeochemical cycles. For example, the 'heavy lifting' of oceanic photosynthesis — global phytoplankton contribute between 50% and 85% of the oxygen in Earth's atmosphere — is by substantial majority down to myriad microscopic 'germs'. So too the cycling of most chemicals. Microbial life plays the overwhelmingly greatest role in breaking down human and other wastes, making constituent substances available to other life forms, building soil structure and fertility, and recycling vital nutrients.

Take away the 'germs', and life would — quite literally — stop.

ECOSYSTEMS WITHIN US ALL

At this point, let's acquaint ourselves a little better with our endobiomes. The endobiome may not be familiar to many of us. Yet, in reality, it is the greater part of us all.

We might recognise that we are indivisible from the natural world for all our biophysical needs — from food, water and air to other material goods and energy —

as are our economies and our wider life fulfilment. However, we are even more intimately connected to the microbial world in terms of the myriad microscopic life forms that live on and within use. Indeed, the majority of cells in our bodies are not even human at all.

It had become accepted wisdom, now often repeated in articles, books and presentations, that microbial cells outnumber human cells in our bodies by a ratio of around ten to one. This, however, was challenged in a rigorous scientific study in 2016,[1] which concluded that there was approximately zero scientific evidence to back this oft-cited factoid beyond a 1970 study considering the contents of the gut. The new study reset the proportion of 1.3 non-human cells to every single human cell in an average human. But this, in itself, is also a remarkable figure. Each of us is not really, by majority, what we may have thought of as 'us' at all. By significant majority, we are made up of 38 million million (or thousand billion) or so microbes, outnumbering our 30 million million (or so) human cells. Even more remarkable is that the health of the microbial ecosystem comprising our endobiomes has a major influence on our overall health, just as much as our dependence on external living systems for breathing, drinking, eating, excreting and stimulation. We have a far higher concentration of bacteria in our guts than in other organs and body parts, but the bugs are not only everywhere upon us. They are also embedded within us.

Analysis of findings from the Human Genome Project reveals that the DNA in the nuclei of our cells comprises around 20,500 actively protein-coding genes.[2] That is obviously a great deal of coded information. However, it would appear that this number of genes may be insufficient to explain all of the biological functions happening in a human body.[3] In fact, a growing number of studies suggest that a significant part of what determines how our bodies function may not be encoded by our own genes at all, but that the rich collective genome of the trillions of microscopic organisms upon and within our bodies plays significant roles in our functioning and wellbeing.[4] Considering just the human gut, the genetic material of the bacteria and viruses found within it encodes something like 3.3 million genes[5] or, in other words, somewhat shy of 1,500 times more genes than are found in human cells. We know that our gut flora not only provides a barrier to pathogenic organisms, but that there is a far deeper symbiotic (mutually beneficial) relationship as microbes break down food into substances that we can more readily absorb as well as synthesising some of the vitamins we subsequently absorb. Furthermore, the gut flora produces hormones

[1] Sender, R., Fuchs, S. and Milo, R. (2016). Revised estimates for the number of human and bacteria cells in the body. *PLOS Biology*. DOI: https://doi.org/10.1371/journal.pbio.1002533.

[2] Clamp, M. *et al.* (2007). Distinguishing protein-coding and noncoding genes in the human genome. *PNAS*, 104(49), pp. 19428–19433. DOI: https://doi.org/10.1073/pnas.0709013104.

[3] Lee, Y.K., Mazmanian, S.K. and Sarkis, K. (2010). Has the microbiota played a critical role in the evolution of the adaptive immune system? *Science*, 330(6012), pp. 1768–1773. DOI: https://doi.org/10.1126/science.1195568.

[4] Konkel, L. (2013). The environment within: exploring the role of the gut microbiome in health and disease. *Environmental Health Perspectives*, 121(9), pp. A276–A281. DOI: https://doi.org/10.1289/ehp.121-a276.

[5] Zhu. B., Wang, W. and Li, L. (2010). Human gut microbiome: the second genome of human body. *Protein and Cell*, 1(8), pp. 718–725. DOI: http://dx.doi.org/10.1007/s13238-010-0093-z.

that affect our internal functions, and thereby appears to function like an additional endocrine organ within our bodies.[6] The metabolic products of bacteria are found not only in our guts, but are pervasive throughout our whole bodies.

The composition of the human gut microbiome changes over time, adapting with diet and in response to our health. However, we know very little about what lives within our digestive tracts. A 2019 scientific study identified almost 2,000 species of bacteria living in the human gut that had yet to be cultured in the laboratory, let alone identified.[7] And bacteria, let us remember, are just one category amongst the diverse range of microorganisms found therein. Another 2017 scientific survey of DNA fragments circulating in the blood concluded that the huge array of microbes living within us is vastly more diverse than was previously known, 99% of that DNA never before been recognised.[8]

Perturbation of the gut flora is linked with a range of inflammatory and auto-immune conditions,[9,10] our gut flora influencing wider dimensions of health and wellbeing perhaps including mood. There is evidence that some may influence not only the gut but also some disorders of the central nervous system.[11] This is the basis for 'probiotic' bacteria, as featured in some health food advertising. We should really think more than twice before popping an antibiotic pill into this life-giving soup of microbes, perhaps killing the 'goose that lays the golden egg' in attacking just one errant gosling. Our attendant microbial entourage may just be crucial for our resilience to diseases of all types.

The health of the endobiome is also the rationale for 'stool transplant', also known as 'fecal microbiota transplant' (FMT), in which fecal bacteria and other microbes are transplanted from the guts of healthy individuals into the guts of patients suffering a range of problems, including infection by pathogenic gut bacteria such as *Clostridium difficile*. In fact, these practices have a long history. Ayurvedic texts dating back more than 3,000 years recommend intake of cow dung and cow urine as a means to address multiple disorders of the digestive system. Fourth-century medical literature from China refers to the use of fecal matter to treat food poisoning and severe diarrhoea. A traditional Bedouin treatment for dysentery is consumption of fresh camel feces. There are many more such records throughout human history of enrichment of the gut microflora as a treatment for a range of disorders.

[6] Clarke, G. *et al.* (2014). Minireview. Gut microbiota: The neglected endocrine organ. *Molecular Endocrinology*, 28(8), pp. 1221–38. DOI: https://doi.org/10.1210/me.2014–1108.

[7] Almeida, A. *et al.* (2019). A new genomic blueprint of the human gut microbiota. *Nature*, 568, pp. 499–504. DOI: https://doi.org/10.1038/s41586-019-0965-1.

[8] Kowarsky, M. *et al.* (2017). Numerous uncharacterized and highly divergent microbes which colonize humans are revealed by circulating cell-free DNA. *PNAS*, 114(36), pp. 9623–9628. DOI: https://doi.org/10.1073/pnas.1707009114.

[9] Quigley, E.M. (2013). Gut bacteria in health and disease. *Gastroenterology and Hepatology*, 9(9), pp. 560–569.

[10] Shen, S. and Wong, C.H.Y. (2016). Bugging inflammation: Role of the gut microbiota. *Clinical and Translational Immunology*, 5(4): e72. DOI: https://doi.org/10.1038/cti.2016.12.

[11] Wang, H., Lee, I-S., Braun, C. and Enck, P. (2016). Effect of probiotics on central nervous system functions in animals and humans: A systematic review. *Journal of Neurogastroenterology and Motility*, 22(4), pp. 589–605. DOI: https://doi.org/10.5056/jnm16018.

WE ARE LEGION

Humanity is, it seems, defined by much more that the limited subset of genes we inherited from the cells of our simian and hominid ancestors. In this regard, we are in many ways similar to the many other organisms with which we share this planet in depending for our wellbeing on intimate relationships with myriad other species. We know, for example, that corals contain algal cells benefiting from nutrients and shelter, repaying the coral polyps with their photosynthetic products. At microscopic scale, the ciliate *Paramecium bursaria* plays host to unicellular green algae in the genus *Chlorella*, these 'pseudochloroplasts' producing sugar molecules that are shared with the host. However, if the ciliate and the *Chlorella* are separated experimentally, both can exist independently albeit that the *Paramecium* will then ingest but not digest *Chlorella* cells to re-establish the symbiotic partnership. Also, many, or perhaps most, rooted plants have a mutually beneficial and often indivisible relationship with specific mycorrhizal fungi associated with their roots that help convert minerals in the soil into forms available to the host plant, many plants also harbouring mutually beneficial fungi and other microbes in other of their parts including their internal tissues. In fact, the diverse chemicals produced by these 'endophytes' may account for many established and novel medicinal, agricultural and industrial benefits generally attributed to the plants themselves. Floral endophytes represent a new frontier in bioprospecting for new drugs. We, it seems, are no different to these other organisms in terms of reliance for our wellbeing on the many 'germs' upon and within us.

It is now widely accepted that microorganisms play many important roles in the lives of plants and animals, with every macroorganism (larger organism) shaped in some way by microorganisms. This ubiquity, and the functional importance of these intimate interrelationships between what we perceive as distinct larger organisms and their associated microorganism assemblages, calls into question how we understand biological individuality. It also raises deeper questions about how natural selection works in practice.[12] The term 'holobiont' has been applied to biological units comprising larger host organisms and their diverse associated microorganisms, raising questions about whether these holobionts are integrated individuals or are made up of cells of discrete but symbiotic life forms.

All of these fascinating observations raise searching questions about how we perceive what 'us' means, and what exactly it is that makes us whole and healthy.

EVOLUTIONARY ORIGINS

Our relationship with germs appears to be even deeper than their deep embedding within our guts and bodies and their roles in healthy metabolism. They are, in fact, what enables our very cells to function.

---

[12] Skillings, D. (2016). Holobionts and the ecology of organisms: Multi-species communities or integrated individuals? *Biology & Philosophy*, 31, pp. 875–892. DOI: https://doi.org/10.1007/s10539-018-9638-y.

One of the great historic scientific discoveries was cell theory, positing that the basic structural unit of living organisms is the cell and that all cells are the progeny of pre-existing cells. The roots of cell theory and the coining of the term 'cell' itself were precipitated by the first recorded observations of Dutchman Antonie van Leeuwenhoek (1632–1723), a pioneer of microscopy in the 17th century. The genesis of cell theory is generally attributed to Robert Hooke (1635–1703), an English natural philosopher, architect and polymath, albeit that cell theory was eventually fully formulated in 1839 through a long process of scientific debate and consensus-building. There is residual dispute that cell theory always hold true as viruses are non-cellular — they basically comprise packages of genetic material (DNA or RNA) — but the fact that viruses cannot exist freely or reproduce without annexing the mechanisms of host cells tends to support the view that they are not, by common definition, living things. As knowledge of cellular structure grew, the dominant theory — certainly the one that I learned at school and university back in the dark ages of the 1960s and 1970s — was that the membrane-bound nucleus of the cell contained genetic material, and the various organelles (structures within cells that perform specific functions) within the cell's cytoplasm carried out important functions at the command of that nuclear genetic material. That is, at least, for 'eukaryotic' cells (cells with a nucleus and organelles both of which are enclosed within membranes), but not for the 'prokaryotic' cells of bacteria and archaea that have no membrane-bound nucleus or organelles.

However, way back in the 1920s, theories arose that these organelles had some semi-autonomous functions within the cells. This theory was, at the time, roundly derided and dismissed as it ran against the dominant, established understanding. It was not until the invention of powerful electron microscopy in the period following the World War II that the internal structure of bacteria began to be revealed and, with it, marked similarities with the structure and functions of cellular organelles including mitochondria. Mitochondria are known as the 'power pack' organelles, found in large numbers in the cytoplasm of most eukaryotic cells. They are the locations in which the biochemical processes of respiration and energy production occur, breaking down complex molecules and oxidising them to release and store energy used in cellular processes. In the 1960s, it was discovered that mitochondria had genetic material independent of the cell's nucleus: mitochondrial DNA.[13,14]

Chloroplasts, membrane-bound organelles that are the sites of photosynthetic processes harnessing light as an energy source to create organic matter from basic carbon dioxide, water and hydrogen resources, are found in virtually all higher plant cells. In 1962, chloroplasts were also found to possess their own DNA.

[13] Nass, M.M. and Nass, S. (1963). Intramitochondrial fibers with DNA characteristics: i. Fixation and electron staining reactions. *Journal of Cell Biology*, 19(3), pp. 593–611. DOI: https://doi.org/10.1083/jcb.19.3.593.

[14] Schatz, G., Haslbrunner, E. and Tuppy, H. (1964). Deoxyribonucleic acid associated with yeast mitochondria. *Biochemical and Biophysical Research Communications*, 15(2), pp. 127–32. DOI: https://doi.org/10.1016/0006-291X(64)90311-0.

Mitochondria vastly enhance the metabolic efficiency of eukaryotic cells. Chloroplasts enable eukaryotic plant cells to manufacture food from sunlight and inorganic materials. The competitive advantages of cells with mitochondria, including plant cells with chloroplasts, are clear, helping them outcompete less favoured organisms and eventually giving rise to the contemporary diversity of microscopic and large eukaryotic plants and animals.

Progressively, a new theory of cellular evolution began to take shape: one of endosymbiosis. Endosymbiosis is a symbiotic theory of cell evolution, positing that diverse microbial organisms have over time formed progressively deeper symbiotic relationships, eventually becoming fully integrated as the cellular structure of organelles in the eukaryotic cells that make up all visible life forms that we know today. The idea of 'symbiogenesis', suggesting that eukaryotic cells arose from deepening symbiotic relationships between prokaryotic organisms, was first articulated in 1905 and 1910 by Russian botanist Konstantin Mereschkowski. However, Lynn Margulis can take the greatest credit for developing and also popularising the then still radical idea that eukaryotic cells evolved through a series of symbiotic partnerships involving several different kinds of prokaryotic cells, supported by microscopic evidence from 1967. Evidence has progressively gathered to enable the theory of endosymbiosis to become established, with growing support since the 1970s. Most, if not all, organelles in complex cells have some form of structure with analogues in free-living bacteria or archaea.

The same advantages are enjoyed by those coral polyps today in which algal cells become embedded. The phenomenon of coral bleaching — when algal cells are ejected from within the polyp as seas warm — demonstrates the disadvantages of this symbiosis ceasing. The case of the microscopic ciliate *Paramecium bursaria*, playing host to unicellular *Chlorella* algal cells as 'pseudochloroplasts', is perhaps a further example of this symbiotic partnership prior to complete endosymbiosis.

Our knowledge of cell structure and processes evolved from a simpler understanding of cell theory to an idea that, even at our most basic cellular level, we and all higher life forms are in fact little more than a bunch of cohabiting 'germs'. It is a humbling perspective from which to re-evaluate our place in this world and our, formerly, perceived dominion over 'lower' life forms.

PUTTING GERMS TO WORK

We humans have invented all sorts of advanced technologies. However, many are founded on putting to work various microbial 'germs' and the processes they perform.

In sewage treatment, contemporary mainstay technologies include trickling filter beds, rotating biological contactors, activated sludge and wetland systems. All, in reality, are means to enhance microbial contact with biochemically enriched wastewater such that a diversity of flagellates, bacteria, protozoa, archaea, fungi and other microscopic organisms in biofilms or in suspension can get to work oxidising or otherwise converting polluting substances into safer constituents. We deploy various microscopic fungi in fermentation of alcohol, the production of bread, dairy products such as cheese and yoghurt, flavourings and vinegar. We synthesise some commodity substances such as citric acid, amino acids, industrial enzymes and monosodium glutamate through the controlled action of a range of other 'germs'. We harvest from them antibiotic and other drugs, albeit that many are then subsequently synthesised artificially making use of the ingenious chemical strategies evolved by some microbes over evolutionary timescales to ward off other microorganisms. We also use attenuated microbes or their toxins as vaccines, promoting our immune systems to respond to particular pathogens. We even use some 'germs' for controlling pests, such as the wilful spread of myxomatosis (the *Myxoma* virus) to control rabbit populations in the middle decades of the 20th century.

Anaerobic microorganisms can also convert biomass into useful biofuel energy sources, principally through anaerobic fermentation processes producing methane-rich 'biogas' or bioethanol. Photosynthetic bacteria or algae can also be harnessed to produce new biomass that may then be converted into forms serving as energy carrier fuels or even as food.

Microorganisms have been variously put to use by humans for so many beneficial purposes throughout our history — the list of utilities they serve is far too long to list exhaustively — since way back before we even knew they existed.

FOR THE LOVE OF GERMS

It is worth exploring briefly the etymology of the everyday word 'germ'. The word, it seems, emerged in late Middle English via the Old French from the Latin *'germen'*, meaning 'seed' or 'sprout'. This is the root of contemporary words such as 'germinate' and the 'germ' of an idea. Also of the word 'germane', arising in the 17th century from the Anglo-French 'germain' or 'german' with a literal meaning of 'springing from the same parents'. All good positive stuff, and perhaps a more apposite articulation of the myriad good things that 'germs' do, and how utterly reliant we are upon all but a vanishingly small proportion of them that may turn pathogenic.

The provocative *99.9% of All Known Germs* title of this chapter is double-edged. It firstly highlights the undeservedly bad press that germs enjoy. (A statistical corollary of the cleaning product manufacturers' claims is, of course, that one in a thousand will get you anyway!) The second sense is what is described as 'The vast unknown microbial biosphere'[15]: we simply do not know how many species of microbial life exist on Earth. Best guesses, albeit massively uncertain, suggest something in the order of 10^{12} (a million million). So, '99.9% of all germs are unknown' would be a massive underestimate, and that is even before we talk about our vanishingly small understanding of the potentially important roles these diverse bugs play in global ecosystems. What we do know is that they are everywhere, doing their thing 24/7, acting as a complex microecosystem the deep importance of which we can barely begin to fathom.

Germs certainly do not deserve the bad reputation we almost uniformly inflict upon them. Not only are we utterly dependent upon them but, at organ, cellular and subcellular levels, we are in fact made up of them!

---

[15] Pedrós-Alió, C. and Manrubia, S. (2016). The vast unknown microbial biosphere. *PNAS*, 113(24), pp. 6585–6587. DOI: https://doi.org/10.1073/pnas.1606105113.

18 For the Love of Worms

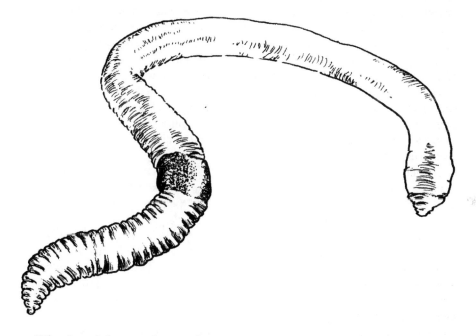

Who doesn't love earthworms?

Let me put that question another way: who wouldn't love earthworms once they appreciated the marvellous things they do that support our security and wellbeing?

WHEN IS A WORM NOT A WORM?

To start with, I should make it clear that I am talking here about earthworms.

True worms form a large group of over 20,000 species of soft-bodied invertebrate animals with annulated (segmented), generally tube-like bodies. These animals are known as the annelids (phylum Annelida). The various species of annelid range in length from under a millimetre to approximately 3 metres, and they are found in most wet environments — both fresh water and marine — through some are parasitic or mutualistic (living in a co-beneficial partnership with other organisms).

Earthworms — the Oligochaetes — are just one amongst other groups of annelids that also include Polychaetes (about 10,000 species of bristleworms found largely in marine environments), Echiura (a small group of marine spoon worms) and Hirudinea (the leeches that are either carnivorous or haemophagic: drinking the blood of other animals). The Oligochaetes comprise some 10,000 species of aquatic and terrestrial worms, including the earthworms found commonly in soil throughout the world where they consume and recycle both living and dead organic matter.

There are in fact many other types of organisms that go by the general term 'worm', and many are not even worms at all.

Other types of 'worms' that are neither earthworms nor true worms include the nematodes, or roundworms (phylum Nematoda). The nematodes are multicellular worms with unsegmented bodies that vary in size from the visible to the microscopic, many of them parasitic (including the pinworms and hookworms that infest the human gut). Nematodes are not closely related to true worms.

The flatworms (phylum Platyhelminthes) are another wide group of 'worms' that are not true worms, divided into four main groups: Turbellaria, Cestoda, Trematoda and Monogenea. Turbellaria are flatworms found in a range of freshwater and terrestrial species, many living non-parasitic predatory and other lifestyles. The other three groups are entirely parasitic groups: the Cestoda are the tapeworms, whereas the Trematoda and Monogenea are known as flukes.

Various elongated beetle larvae are also referred to — inaccurately in biological terms — as 'worms'. Well known amongst them, and retailed as food for birds and fish, is the 'meal worm'. This is the larval form of the meal worm beetle (*Tenebrio molitor*). Silk worms and glow worms too are insects, not true worms.

And then there is the slow worm which is not a worm but is a reptile and, though snake-like, is also not a snake but is a legless lizard. The most common and widely distributed is the common slow worm (*Anguis fragilis*) native to Eurasia. A further species, the Peloponnese slowworm (*Anguis cephalonnica*), is endemic to Greece. These lizards have lost their legs, though the vestigial structures are still found within their bodies.

There is even, allegedly, a type of dragon known as a Wurm, also variously spelled by those that spell such things as Worm, Orm, Vurm or Wyrm. Both as a scientist and as, I am guessing, one amongst many of us who has never seen a wurm, I am not able to verify the biology of these mythical creatures. However, it is told by those that tell such things that wurms are a type of dragon that takes the form of a serpent with coils that can wrap around hills and bodies. It is said that a wurm can be mistaken for solid earth, and that it may be appropriately rather large. The head of the wurm is reported to be shaped variously like that of a horse or a crocodile, sometimes with horns, dangerously large fangs, and bright, wide eyes. They are reportedly found in swamps, marshes, and other dank or wet places — like many types of wetland unfairly ascribed negative connotations — as well as forests and lonely places, and may also make their homes in lakes or even wells. The wurm's reported common geographical distribution is the United Kingdom, France and elsewhere across Western Europe. Wurms are also able, like their mythical kin the other types of dragon, to exhale fire and noxious fumes, and also to move at incredible speed. However, unlike other alleged dragon types, wurms lack redeeming qualities and are wholly malicious and destructive towards people. Given they (probably) don't exist, that is in fact quite an exhaustive set of details about this mythical beast!

Now that we have got those lessons in taxonomy and mythology out of the way, let's talk about the fascinating inner world of the earthworm.

HEALTHY SOILS NEED HEALTHY EARTHWORMS

Healthy soils need healthy earthworm populations. Worms draw down organic matter from the surface into underlying soil strata, bringing with them nutrient chemicals. They contribute to decomposition processes, both directly by digesting organic matter and indirectly by drawing it into the soil where other small life forms can get to work on it, converting complex matter into simpler substances useful to a huge diversity of soil organisms and rooted plants.

Through their actions, and that of the other microscopic and larger beasts sharing the soil with them, earthworms rebuild the soil's tilth and fertility. This benefits not only the whole soil ecosystem but also everything that grows within and from it. Other creatures eat plants nourished by fertile soils, these herbivores are in turn eaten by carnivores so forming a key part of the great planetary cycles of chemicals and energy. Without the generally unseen activities of earthworms, much of this planet-wide system would struggle to function, if not collapse entirely.

The importance of earthworms to farming, the water cycle and wider biodiversity can't be over-estimated. Without worms, our soil would be seriously degraded, less fertile and necessitate greater energy and chemical inputs with associated financial costs to produce the food and fibre commodities that form the basis of many economic activities as well as food security.

HEALTHY WATER ALSO NEEDS HEALTHY EARTHWORMS

Through their burrowing activities, worms also make major, vital contributions to oxygenation and the permeability of soils. Take away the burrowing worms and soils would become increasingly compacted, water infiltrating downwards at substantially slower rates. Instead, much of the water that falls as rain would rush off the land surface, increasing rates of soil surface erosion and exacerbating downstream flood risk.

Furthermore, the replenishment of underlying groundwater would be seriously compromised. Not only would this contribute to water shortages and reduce drought resilience but, as groundwater is naturally filtered and therefore cheaper to treat when extracted for human uses, greater expense and chemical and energy inputs would be incurred in treating more poorly filtered water extracted for human uses. So, earthworms help us in a surprisingly direct way in averting both flood and drought risks as well as spiralling water service bills.

HEALTHY ECOSYSTEMS NEED HEALTHY EARTHWORMS

Aside from their contributions to nutrient and energy cycling, earthworms are also tasty and nutritious morsels in their own right. Maybe they are not seen as such by all of us humans.

Earthworms are known as the 'blackbird's favourite', providing important food for many birds from blackbirds and thrushes to buzzards and kites. Blackbirds are in fact one amongst many types of bird that undertake 'worm charming', trampling the soil surface to emulate rain such that worms rise up to the surface and can be picked off by the cunning bird. Other bird species, particularly waders such as the Northern lapwing (*Vanellus vanellus*), probe moist soil to feed on a variety of worms, insects and small crustaceans, all of these food sources often limited by increasing farming intensity and agrochemicals. Robins (*Erithacus rubecula*) are also 'The gardener's friend' as they follow gardeners around closely as they turn the soil exposing worms and other tasty morsels, commonly perching on a fork handle or adjacent branch in anticipation and commonly nesting in watering cans or similar shelter in potting sheds. In the wild, robins will also follow wild boar and other animals that turn the soil, becoming their 'friends' too, just as they become quite tame where recreational angling is popular and where they learn to beg for titbits of maggot or worm.

Badgers too forage for worms, particularly in winter when other food is scarce, as do foxes, shrews and voles. Worms also are the mainstay of moles, which seek them out in moist soils. In central Africa, bonobos (also known as pygmy chimpanzees) and gorillas regularly eat earthworms.

And, as many an angler knows, a huge diversity of fish species from the smallest stickleback to the mightiest salmon can't resist a juicy earthworm!

EATING EARTHWORMS

Whilst we noted that earthworms may not be seen as tasty and nutritious morsels by all of us humans, this is in fact a very 'developed world' perspective. We in industrialised society might regard worms as disgusting and inedible, yet various types of worms, grubs and insects are welcomed as nutritious and delicious types of food in various other parts of the world. All earthworm species are in fact edible by humans.

Māori people in New Zealand consider earthworms a delicacy, as do people in the Fujian and Guangdong provinces of China. The Ye'kuana Amerindian people in southern Venezuela gather them from the moist earth around streams or on the highland forest floor, the earthworms when gutted and either boiled or smoked forming a major part of the diet. Worms are also key parts of the diet in various regions of Africa, New Guinea and other parts of South America. Though not widespread, fried earthworms added to ramen have been a feature of some Japanese restaurants. In the Philippines, the earthworm species *Perionyx excavatus* species was bred in vegetable waste and then processed with herbs and seasoning to make steaklets for humans to eat in the early 1980s, although, when the source of this food became known, it did not prove popular. Other recipes found on the internet include fried earthworms and worm-based candied jerky.

Before moving on from the wonderful world of earthworm gastronomy, we have to touch upon the widely discussed but wholly fallacious urban myth that the McDonald's chain, and the Wendy's chain before that, made hamburgers with ground earthworm filler. Though many of us of a certain age will have known about this when the rumours were flowing, there is neither a shred of evidence nor truth in the rumours. In fact, way back in the 1970s, McDonald's founder Ray Kroc explained that a pound of worms cost more than twice as much as a pound of ground beef, making it an illogical filler choice even if the potential reputational damage were not enough to make it a stupid idea.

In fact, adding earthworms to the human diet is not such a mad idea, at least not to the many people who do not live within the narrower world view of the Western, industrialised world. After all, earthworms are in many ways a 'superfood', readily foraged and very efficiently grown on organic waste. When cleaned, they comprise as much as 82% protein and carry high levels of iron and other metals, amino acids and other valuable dietary additions. What's not to like?

PUTTING EARTHWORMS TO WORK

Cultivation of worms is known as vermiculture, serving the three functions of re-cycling of organic waste, production of rich fertiliser and the harvesting of worms. Worms have been very widely used in resource management and waste manage-ment throughout human history. The presence and activities of these earthworms may have been purely fortuitous, as in the case of earthworms finding their way into and proliferating in leaf piles and compost heaps and so contributing to their breakdown and transformation into useful resources. But, increasingly, earthworms such as the brandling (*Eisenia fetida*) have been actively used in industrial vermiculture-based waste management systems converting large volumes of factory farm and other organic wastes into a friable, odourless material useful as a fertiliser and soil conditioner. A further benefit of these industrial-scale solutions is that the earthworms may be sold on for various applications such as food for fish, bait for recreational angling, as well as a high-protein food supplement for pet and farmed poultry. Experimental feeding of pigs on feed supplemented with brandlings found that they offered a nutritional boost. In Kenya, other earthworm species bred on vegetable mulch are used to feed farmed *Tilapia* fish. When staying with friends in Sweden, I found that they and their neighbours had home-scale wormeries also using brandlings to break down their domestic organic waste, disposing benignly of the digested remains on open land.

The 'NiiMi process' is still relatively common in rural Japan, in part making use of worms for purifying household waste water. The NiiMi process takes the form of a capillary siphon trench, a soil-based wastewater disposal system similar to con-ventional septic tank leaching field trenches, except that the trenches are filled with capillary sand instead of gravel and the lower quarter of the trench is lined with an impermeable membrane. The flow of wastewater through the upper, unsaturated and aerated soil profile stimulates biological activity that contributes to the removal of organic and nutrient matter.

Various traditional medicinal applications of earthworms are found around the world, covering everything from human gut ailments to treatments for haemor-rhoids, as a hair restorer and as an aphrodisiac. I have to confess that I have not tried any of them!

GETTING TO KNOW OUR EARTHWORMS

There are 25 species of earthworms in Britain. There are many more than that in the United States, the roster of earthworms there also including various European species introduced by settlers from the beginning in the 16th century probably in soil used as ballast on ships or on the root balls of plants. Globally, there are thought to be around 6,000–10,000 earthworm species. Some are aquatic, but many live in terrestrial soils preferring some moisture, including in floodplains but also on higher grounds where they burrow downwards to follow the water in dry conditions.

Britain's largest earthworm is the lobworm (*Lumbricus terrestris*), or 'common earthworm'. Lobworms can be up to 12 centimetres (nearly 5 inches) long, living in vertical burrows up to 3 metres (9 feet) deep from which they emerge at night to feed on fallen leaves and other decaying plant material and to mate with adjacent worms. This same species is known as the nightcrawler in the United States and also the dew worm or grandaddy earthworm in Canada, though lobworms are in fact an introduced species in the Americas, first arriving with European settlers.

Britain's many smaller worm species include the often red-and-yellow striped brandling worm (*Eisenia fetida*) found commonly in compost and other moist de-caying leaf litter, organic-rich soils and manure heaps. Also, the hardy, banded reddish-brown dendrobaena (or 'European nightcrawler', *Eisenia hortensis*), usually found in woodland litter and soils rich in organic matter. The dendrobaena is popular as an angling bait, but also increasingly used in composting.

There are many more British worm species. There is even an Earthworm Society of Britain[1] that aims to promote and support scientific research about earthworms, their environments and their conservation.

WONDERFUL WORMS

A persistent myth, still often repeated, is that, if you cut a worm in two, each half will regenerate into a new worm. In reality, cutting a worm in half results simply in a dead worm! Though apparently simple, worms are in fact complex organisms with a mouth at the front, a long gut to extract organic matter from ingested soil and decaying vegetation, an anus at the rear with associated vascular, reproductive and other organs *en route*. They will no more regenerate when cut in half as will you or I!

The Ancient Greek philosopher Aristotle (384–322 BC) called earthworms the 'earth's guts' as they act like intestines by processing the soil's organic matter and turning it into food for plants. This is in fact a fair appellation for these great servants of global ecosystems. The Egyptian Queen Cleopatra (69–30 BC) also recognised the great contribution made by humble earthworms to Egyptian agri-culture, declaring them by law to be sacred.

Earthworms do all sorts of amazing things in ecosystems, in our diets, in other human uses from waste processing to recreational angling and agricultural pro-duction, even in medicine, philosophy and gastronomy. Without them, the world might just stop working.

So, who now doesn't love earthworms?

---

[1] https://www.earthwormsoc.org.uk/.

19 The Ecology of Space Travel

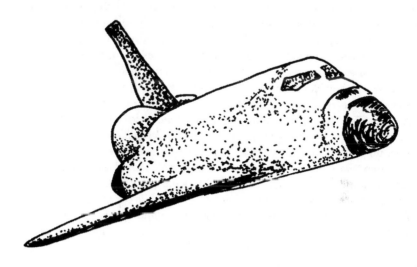

On 21st July 1969, I was quite tired. You see, although I was still in the final year of primary school, I was permitted to sit up deep into the preceding night to watch live television coverage of Neil Armstrong and 'Buzz' Aldrin landing the Apollo 11 lunar module on the moon and then, at 2:56 in the morning (UK time), to see Armstrong taking his *'One small step for man'* to disturb the grey dust of the lunar surface. It was thrilling, epoch-defining, awe-inspiring, and it filled us with pride at the ingenuity that characterises our species and which had now enabled us to make that '... *one giant leap for mankind'*.

It would be untrue to say that this event steered me into science and the study of ecosystems and our interdependence with them. Indeed, I had an uncontrollable passion for all things aquatic from far earlier in my childhood memories. But there was, in that window of history, a palpable zeitgeist of excitement about the seemingly limitless bounds of science and technology, not to mention the deep impact that many of us felt on seeing that first image of 'Earthrise' as our tiny blue planet rose over the lunar horizon. Back in those heady ways, the reputation of technology had not yet been shadowed by the controversies with which we are familiar today, ranging from climate change to acid rain, genetically modified organisms (GMOs), 'Frankenstein foods' and uncontrolled nanotechnology, synthetic biology and accumulations of persistent plastic as well as electronic waste.

THE ASCENT OF HUMANITY

Humanity's ascent from hunter-gatherer to settled civilisation has been substantially characterised by evolving technological means in a transition from merely harvesting to harnessing nature. A key element of this 9,000-year journey has been control of water. It was this innovation that created the opportunity for evolution of societies freed by cultivation and animal husbandry from the daily drudgery of securing fresh food. Control of water systems for irrigation, transport, power, cooling and a host of other uses, exploitation of the energy content of wood, coal and radioactive substances, and the use of various natural resources both as raw and as highly processed materials have all been a feature of humanity's ascending technological sophistication and capabilities. This has placed us apart from the other animals with which we share a common home planet and ancestry.

As a consequence, a sense of superiority over nature has been prevalent throughout much of the recorded history of the Western world. As long ago as the time of writing of Genesis 1:28 in the (King James version of the) Bible, God was purported to have blessed the humans He had created with the exhortation to '... *Be fruitful, and multiply, and replenish the earth, and subdue it: and have dominion over the fish of the sea, and over the fowl of the air, and over every living thing that moveth upon the earth*'. There are other interpretations of this text in its original Hebrew relating more to good stewardship of the Earth, and contemporary directions such as the encyclical letter *Laudato Si* issued by Pope Frances in 2015 is explicit about humanity's duties to care for 'our common home'.[1] Many other faiths across the planet and throughout history also reference duties of care towards Earth's supporting ecosystems, including their framing as part of a creation. Nonetheless, we have certainly been pretty good at 'subduing' and 'having dominion' and, regarding our fruitfulness, well in excess of 7.7 billion bipeds now trample across every continent and trade resources between them. Our technological capabilities have reached the point of diverting whole river systems across subcontinents, and unleashing atomic power in devices potent and numerous enough to expunge all life from the face of the planet. We have even put people not only into space, but upon the face of another world some quarter of a million miles distant from our own. But it would be a case of misplaced arrogance to consider ourselves as in any way other than an integral part of nature.

NO PLACE LIKE OUR HOME PLANET

Wherever we venture in the universe, we need to eat, drink and breathe. We are of terrestrial origin and co-evolved with the ecosystems that sustain us, and would do well to remember that this is so in all of our innovations and decisions. Consequently, even when we travel up into the thin upper atmosphere or beyond it, we have to use technological means to take the planet's resources with us. These sophisticated life support systems, referred to by NASA (the US National Aeronautic and Space Administration) and other space interests as Environmental Control and Life Support Systems (ECLSS), are essential for supplying these three basic resources — solid, liquid and gaseous substances — and for dealing with the wastes that arise from their

---

[1] Pope France. (2015). Encyclical letter *Laudato Si'* of the Holy Father Francis on care for our common home. (https://earthministry.org/wp-content/uploads/2015/05/Laudato-Si.pdf, accessed 7 June 2020.)

use. ECLSS technology also maintains equable temperature and air pressure and shields us from the intense radiation from space once we are no longer cossetted by the planet's natural stratospheric shields, a miraculous system maintained by close interaction with the very life forms it protects and which we perhaps take for granted to the extent of not thinking about how marvellous that fact is.

Even in space, we need a combined daily mass of around 5 kg of food, water and oxygen, and for systems to deal with the equivalent weight of waste matter that inevitably arises in solid, liquid and gaseous forms including solid biological wastes such as hair, fingernails and flakes of skin.[2] On Earth, we take for granted the biological systems that do all of these things with such wonderful efficiency. But, in space, all of the water must not only be stored but also efficiently reclaimed after use, which of course means that it must be recaptured after leaving the body as urine, moisture in feces, sweat and in our outbreaths. We have yet to devise a workable plant cultivation system enabling food to be grown from our solid waste when in space, though natural processes captured by constructed wetland systems and composting toilets can recover nutrient matter for reuse on Earth. This means that food must be packaged for storage and consumption during space flight. Likewise, the air has to be refreshed and cleansed, including reinjection of oxygen and safe absorption of carbon dioxide and other trace gases.

Every one of the 536 people from 38 countries who had gone into space by 2013, of which only 24 have travelled beyond low Earth orbit,[3] have had to take with them a compressed source of home atmosphere or else technical means to regenerate it. We are integral to the Gaian bubble into which we were born and which has shaped our bodies and psychologies just as we, as cogs in the marvellously complex 'machine' of the biosphere, inevitably shape the biosphere and all of the living and non-living things that share it.

Without these technological, Earth-emulating processes, all of course powered by energy derived from terrestrial sources and topped up by solar energy emulating the processes of plant leaves, life outside of the thin skin of air surrounding our home planet is impossible. And the same principles apply equally to the Primary Life Support Systems (PLSSs) devised in space suits, whether as standalone systems or as umbilically connected to spacecraft during space walks.

The key point here is not the diversity and sophistication of the technologies, but that all such technologies are simply innovative means to plumb us into the ecosystems upon which we are inextricably dependent. We can extend this dependence through technological means, but we can never break it. After all, irreparable brain damage sets in if a person is deprived of air for anything beyond four minutes; without replenishing our bodies with fresh water, we are

---

[2] Sulzman F.M. and Genin, A.M. (1994). *Space, Biology, and Medicine, Vol. II: Life Support and Habitability*. American Institute of Aeronautics and Astronautics: Washington, DC. DOI: https://doi.org/10.2514/4.104664.

[3] As of 6 November 2013, according to Fédération Aéronautique Internationale criteria which defines spaceflight as any flight over 100 kilometres (62 miles) altitude. (Source: Wikipedia: http://en.wikipedia.org/wiki/List_of_space_travelers_by_name, accessed 26 May 2020.)

likely to die after only four days depending on climate; and without food, death ensues after around 40 days. Our survival needs are so hard-wired into us by evolution that it is impossible to kill ourselves by holding our breath, as we saw in Chapter 7, *A Breath of Fresh Air*. It is all the more surprising that we take our fundamental ecological dependencies so much for granted in the ways we live our conscious lives.

BREAKING THE LIFE SUPPORT MACHINE

For much of our technological history, humanity has not merely overlooked the central importance of nature but has seemingly waged war upon it. We have, for example, erected flood walls to keep water out of the floodplains it has carved out in the landscape, blaming nature when the things we then build on these natural habitats are inundated during excessive river flows or when water is no longer able to dissipate across broad river valleys but is instead accelerated downstream to swamp towns and farmland. We spray chemicals to deter the growth of plant species that compete with those we favour, or to kill insects and other species that graze upon them, effectively appropriating virtually the entire productive potential of landscapes for our own ends. Our species appropriates nearly one quarter of total planetary primary production for our own ends.[4] We also wonder why problems such as failing pollination, soil erosion and health impacts come back to bite us. We now also re-engineer water flows across entire continents, most extremely to date in China's massive water diversion projects that stem the flow of the Yangtze River to redirect it northwards into the Yellow River basin, creating structures such as the Three Gorges Dam which are heavy enough to measurably alter the tilt of the Earth's axis and stimulate earthquakes.[5] Miraculous medical advances have dramatically increased the longevity of those in the developed world, skewing the incidence of disease from those associated with inadequate to excessive consumption, yet at the same time desensitising humanity to the inevitability and naturalness of death.

Worst of all, we have created a market economy that depends entirely on what nature does for us yet values very little of it, with a roster of destructive impacts that inevitably return to blight our collective prospects for continuing to live healthy, profitable and fulfilled lives. And, by tacitly declaring this conceptual and economic apartheid between us and nature, we cut ourselves off from the very roots that nourish our future security and potential. Yet, even at our most technologically advanced, even in spaceships flying to the moon and one day perhaps to Mars and even beyond, our biological dependency remains unbreakable.

---

[4] Haberl, H. *et al.* (2007). Quantifying and mapping the human appropriation of net primary production in earth's terrestrial ecosystems. *PNAS*, 104(31), pp. 12942–12947. DOI: https://doi.org/10.1073/pnas. 0704243104.

[5] Everard M. (2013). *The Hydropolitics of Dams: Engineering or Ecosystems?* London: Zed Books.

SPACESHIP EARTH

We engineer metal, plastics and energy from reserves laid down by natural processes in the Earth's crusts to enable these 'giant leaps for mankind', yet the spaceship itself is a microcosm of our own lives here on Earth. The term 'Spaceship Earth' was coined by Henry George in 1879 describing our home planet as '... *a well-provisioned ship, this on which we sail through space. If the bread and beef above decks seem to grow scarce, we but open a hatch and there is a new supply, of which before we never dreamed. And very great command over the services of others comes to those who as the hatches are opened are permitted to say, "This is mine!"*'[6]

Various allusions to Spaceship Earth since the middle 1960s have brought the term into more common parlance, defining a world view that recognises this planet as a system of renewable yet finite resources suspended in space. In microcosm, burning plastics to generate heat in the space shuttle would yield one aspect of benefit but at devastating cost to the air, water and other systems supporting the lives of its inhabitants. So too, at a grander scale, the wellbeing of Spaceship Earth requires of the more technologically capable and populous species amongst its 'crew' a high degree of harmonious cooperation informed by the workings of the spaceship, its management directed to contribute to a greater and long-term good.

Dire prognoses and suggested changes in strategy and technology are the meat and drink of most writers and campaigners on environment and sustainability matters, and I count myself amongst that band of voices often sounding into the wilderness. And real 'joined up' and ecologically literate policy reform with associated shifts in governance, fiscal measures and technology are urgently needed. However, that is not the point of this little book. This volume is about the important first steps of recognition and appreciation of how we are rooted in the beneficence of nature, and will share inevitably in both its fortunes and fates.

NATURE IS AN EVERY EVERYDAY THING

Nature is as integral to space flight as it is to my mug of tea, my tatty old tee-shirts and the air that you and I breathe as we read a newspaper that is both derived from and will return to be reintegrated into the cycles of the natural world. The plastic dashboard and metal bodywork of my car are merely temporary forms created through human ingenuity from substances laid down in the Earth's crust by natural processes operating over hundreds of millions of years. They will return to the living system after the tenure in my ownership of that vehicle which, like my whole life, is less than a blink in the eye of geological time.

Nature is, in short, as much all around us in space flight as it is in all other facets of our lives, within and running through us every second of our days and in all the things that surround us. We need to recognise this, value it, and live our lives enriched and informed by this knowledge to underwrite a future of security and opportunity.

---

[6] George, H. (1879). *Progress and Poverty: An Enquiry into the Cause of Industrial Depressions and of Increase of Want with Increase of Wealth — The Remedy.* Doubleday, Page and Company: New York. (Quote from book IV, chapter 2.)

20 On Safari without Leaving the House

Isn't it great to get away from it all into wild spaces? Just ourselves in the rawness of nature, the experience shared with a select chosen group of special people. It is exhilarating to feel the force of wind harnessed by and straining at the sails of a small boat, to sense the lap of water around our toes as we paddle or above our heads as we scuba dive, to view an imposing vista from a hill or mountain, or to experience another expansive panorama. It is a wonder to see heaven or hell etched in a cloudscape, and to witness the kaleidoscope of living things both great and small that populate every niche from the microscopic to the oceanic in their profusion and diversity.

NATURE AT HOME

Yet pausing a moment to reflect — perhaps whilst nursing a cup of tea or a bowl of rice, lying in the bath, pulling on a tee-shirt, reading a newspaper, pausing for breath or musing about space travel — it is invigorating and exhilarating to connect with the reality that nature is not merely something remotely 'out there' in the special places to which we escape all too rarely. Rather, nature is not only all around us in those familiar things with which we have perhaps grown too familiar, but is inside us and passing through us each and every moment. We are, and will always remain, indivisible and wholly interdependent elements of a natural world with which we evolved, and which continues unflinchingly to support our needs and demands within the bounds of its capabilities.

A quick safari around the house will confirm the pervasive presence of nature in the materials and energy from which these everyday things are made and which maintain them, and the places and processes that will re-assimilate them once again as wastes, ultimately regenerating them over a range of timescales into fresh resources. Nature is there in the carpet, in the paint, the kitchen table and the cutlery. It's in the television and the computer if we just look a little closer, including in all of their components from transistors and glass, wires and plastics. It is the food in our cupboards, including the jars, bottles, boxes and packets in which it is stored. It is the source and recipient of the soap, the shampoo and the numerous lotions and potions in the bathroom.

We could go on and on with examples of nature's ubiquity in the commonplace, but the point is made. Dig down into the details of all the everyday things around us and each will reveal their own fascinating ecology, and indeed their relative transience in that current form: a mere ephemeral configuration of natural resources passing through eternal cycles. Each element comes from and goes back to nature, and all the flows into and out from our lives and living spaces have deep biological, geochemical, environmental, economic, cultural, political and spiritual ramifications. And so we are all unbreakably connected with the natural world and, via that, also one to another, sharing a common, inseparable destiny

HUMAN NATURE

Though in our basic biology we are an indivisible element of nature, we differ both qualitatively and quantitatively from other life forms in terms of our capacities to manipulate nature to serve our own ends. Like no other species, we have modified landscapes, rivers and water flows, seascapes and the Earth's crust to produce food, energy, metals, aggregates and other materials, and then proceeded to make clever things with them from which people (at least in the developed world) have benefitted massively. Consequently, we surround and cosset ourselves with everyday things that, despite our familiarity with them, are revealed by a little reflection to be, in their own different ways, quite miraculous.

The constitution of each of the everyday things that make our modern lives comfortable illustrates the genius of human ingenuity entailed in bending natural matter and energy flows into forms that serve our needs and desires. Thus, we emancipate ourselves from excesses of cold, heat, hunger, predation, parasitism, storm and darkness whilst, in a purely biological sense, being no way apart from the rest of nature. If we overlook this fundamental connectedness then our health is likely to suffer, and our activities are more likely to inflict harm upon ecosystems that are fundamental for the continuing wellbeing of all. And all this through a cardinal sin not of intent but of omission: that of too frequently overlooking how it is always nature that provides the goods and pays the bills of our lifestyles, their associated demands on resources and their legacy of waste materials.

This book is not about 'heavy environmentalist' messages related to the trajectory of the developed world, the burgeoning global human population and its conflict with the precipitous decline in nature's spaces and integrity, nor the grave implications of these pressures for climate stability, pollution, resource depletion and inequities inflicted upon those sharing this Earth, now and into the future. These things are of course vitally important, and need our urgent attention if we are to secure prospects to live a decent quality of life into the future. Instead, this book is concerned with the first and most important objective of looking afresh and learning to appreciate how nature is within and around us always, from 'natural' places and spaces right through to the most extreme expressions of our technological prowess. At the core of this book is just how deeply we humans are indivisibly embedded within and dependent upon the living world, even within our most extreme technical sophistication from massive water management schemes that span whole subcontinents to our supercomputers, foodstuffs, clothing and spacecraft.

So, pause another moment to reflect. Spend a while enjoying the safari of everyday things without even leaving the house, or indeed shifting from the sofa.

When we feel that kind of connectedness with the natural world that spawned and continues to support us, we touch something important about what it is to be a human being intimately interconnected with this amazing planet and the many other living things that share it. We also then need to give pause to reflect on the need to steer the human journey on a more symbiotic pathway, such that nature can continue to nurture us and provide us with security and opportunity into the future.

A rewarding 'safari' indeed, and all without leaving the house!

21 Living on a Planet

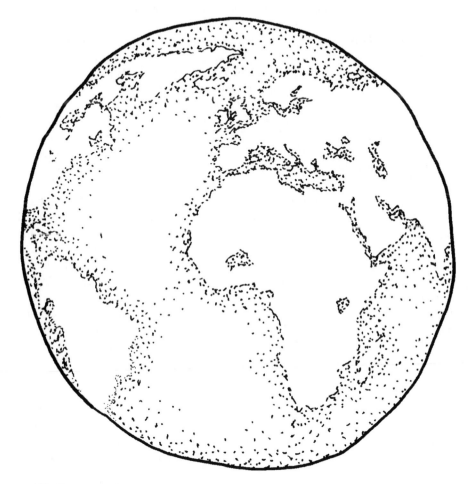

We live on a planet.

This may not be the most revelatory of utterances. It is also difficult to argue otherwise. (Unless, that is, you are an academic as we tend to contest everything, such as exactly what is meant by 'live', 'we', 'planet', 'on' and possibly even 'a', but let's just content ourselves for now that even academics tend to suffer poor health prospects when stranded in deep space rather than in the maternal embrace of this small, blue planet.) However, for all the certainty encompassed by that succinct five-word sentence, the full implications of living on a planet remain at best only partially reflected in the everyday ways we think and act.

As in a spaceship, everything that we consume — by mouth, lung or passive absorption — has to have come from our immediate surroundings. So too, everything we excrete — as feces, urine, sweat, moist breath, skin flakes, detached hairs, bits of toenail and so forth — becomes part of those same immediate surroundings. And that machine, be it a living planet or the engineering wonder that is a spaceship, has also to detoxify, re-assimilate, regenerate or sequester, removing the stuff that does us harm and recreating the stuff we need.

The contemporary space race has been proceeding in earnest since the late 1950s. Planet Earth's amazing, internally interdependent life support mechanism has a head start of 3.85 billion years. However, exactly the same rules apply. Put the wrong stuff into our surroundings — stuff like organochlorine pesticides that are novel to nature and which living cells therefore lack the mechanism to break down safely, or else stuff like mined metals and phosphorus released today in such volumes that they overwhelm nature's re-assimilative capacities — and bad things will or are likely to happen. Likewise, disable the living 'machinery' of nature, and all of those things it does seamlessly — so seamlessly in fact that we take them mainly for granted — are going to become degraded. This may manifest across a spectrum from the catastrophic collapse of a fishery, loss of croplands to salinisation, poisoning of an aquifer or the demise of any other productive system, through to more nuanced degradation such as incremental loss of insects or other crucial biodiversity, or increasing atmospheric carbon dioxide concentrations. All erode the resilience of ecosystems and their capacities to secure our needs into the future.

What is an acceptable level of loss of natural food productivity, photosynthesis and soil regeneration? How much is an acceptable decline in pollination, primary production or natural purification of air and water? What is a tolerable limit to impoverishment of humanity's opportunity to live culturally enriched lives, or be subject to incremental increases in risks from pollution, flood, disease or fire? How many cut strands in the web of life, evolved adaptively and flexibly over billions of years, constitute a genuinely negligible degree of harm? What is the legacy of the largely unrecognised ramifications of day-to-day contemporary lifestyle demands for the ecosystems vital for our continuing security and opportunity, regardless of our best intentions?

It matters that we know about the ecology of everyday things. With the pressures of 7.7 billion resource-hungry bipeds today, augmented by 2–3 billion more mouths and heavy pairs of feet by 2050, we have to learn that the collective weight of our lifestyle demands cannot continue indefinitely, or indeed for much longer, to outweigh the finite and already sharply declining capacities of the ecosystems of Planet Earth. Reconnecting with the ecological realities of everyday things offers not merely enlightenment, but also an enlightening route towards rethinking a more sustainable future.

THE GIFT OF CONSCIOUSNESS

Today, we suffer the double-edged sword of apparent emancipation from a natural world too often caricatured solely as being 'red in tooth and claw', as famously coined by Alfred Lord Tennyson.[1] Some even celebrate our perceived dominance over nature, as in the massive flood walls, large dams, tidal defence schemes

---

[1] Canto 56, Alfred Lord Tennyson's *In Memoriam A. H. H.*, 1850.

and plans for geoengineering that embody a sense of 'taming' natural forces. But, perhaps more commonly, it is our degree of ignorance that signals our greatest disconnection from the Earth's intimately co-evolved ecosystems that remain ever active in supporting all dimensions of our modern lives and their associated demands. Rediscovering and celebrating that natural connection in everyday things is what this book is fundamentally all about.

The last thing I want to do is to depress you about our footprint on the Earth's resources, and its implications for our own continuity. After all, bumblebees, larch trees, swallows and fiddler crabs get by without such angst about their rootedness in nature, and their total interdependence with all of the remarkable living and non-living things it comprises. They just get on with life, as must we all.

But one of the ways in which we depart from the rest of the living menagerie of which we are an indivisible part is in our capacities for awareness and foresight about how integrated and co-evolved a cog we are in the marvellous living machinery of the natural world, and also the scale at which our superior cognitive abilities have enabled us to bend natural resources to serve our sole needs. Of course, crows gather twigs to build nests, and crayfish and rabbits dig burrows in the earth for their protection. But our manipulation of planetary systems is at a whole different scale, and one that imperils us if we are not to use that same human ingenuity to find ways to live sustainably, rather than merely just to extend our technological reach without regard for future consequences.

This is the double-edged sword of consciousness enabled by the massive expansion of the human forebrain, which we can use solely for immediate advantage or else deploy with forethought. This differs from the involuntary control of our breathing (as described in Chapter 7, *A Breath of Fresh Air*) that mirrors much of the behaviour of most, though far from all, of the animal kingdom. Our consciousness equips us with the potential for ingenuity that we have deployed largely to date for short-term gain by means generally blind to longer-term ramifications. But consciousness also enables us to learn and consequently to think in more informed and far-sighted ways, aware of and wisely pre-empting negative consequences not only for ourselves but for the ecosystems we all depend upon for our ongoing wellbeing. At this stage of evolution, we understand enough as a species to have to accept responsibility both for innovating and acting in a more far-sighted manner, or alternatively to take the blame for a continuing legacy of continued short-termism for which tomorrow's generations may condemn but cannot sanction us.

The most fundamental step towards this higher use of our consciousness is awareness: awareness of the pervasive nature of our connectedness with the ecosystems within which we co-evolved. From awareness can emerge respect and value, and from these qualities can stem the impetus to live more in synergy with the supporting ecosystems we depend upon now and into the future to underwrite all of our needs and aspirations.

Fundamentally, this book is a celebration of nature, and specifically about how it supports even the smallest everyday things in our everyday lives, even if we have so frequently overlooked it. It is thereby a call to action, to innovate and live more far-sighted, equitable and sustainable lives.

SAYING GRACE

Perhaps, for example, we do not say grace often enough for the food on our table. I am not personally of a religious persuasion, or at least not in a 'party political' sense of organised religion. However, we in the privileged Western world are undoubtedly graced by our ready access to food. It was not ever thus.

In reality, it is only for less than one-tenth of human history that food sufficiency has been taken mainly for granted by rising civilisations. Artefacts from the city of Uruk, centre of the first recorded settled human civilisation on Earth in the 'fertile crescent' between the Tigris and Euphrates rivers in land now lying in modern-day Iraq, reveal a settled society enabled by liberation from the daily drudgery of seeking out food to go on to differentiate labour, social roles and physical infrastructure. The innovation enabling this first civilisation was the manipulation of water flows, and the purloining of selected species of plants and animals to develop settled agriculture so as to free people from hunting and gathering.

Food sufficiency, often allied with manipulation of water resources, has been the basis of all successive civilisations, as we saw, for example, in the often unrecorded or underappreciated history of rice paddy systems constituting vital yet overlooked underpinnings of great recorded civilisations (in Chapter 5, *A Simple Bowl of Rice*). Mismanagement of water resources and their associate solutes has also been a major contributory factor to the subsequent failure of many civilisations. For example, progressive salinisation of soils through irrigation of landscapes with high evaporation rates gradually degraded food productivity in Mesopotamia, as evidenced by documentation of a succession of increasingly salt-tolerant plants species and finally the undermining of the whole culture. By the time British forces occupied the vicinity in 1932, the resident population had declined to levels witnessed prior to the rise of the Mesopotamian civilisation. Similar cycles of food productivity and its successive paucity due to unsustainable management have been contributory to the rise and fall of civilisations as far apart as Easter Island in the Pacific through to Greenland in the Arctic Circle.[2]

The food on our tables that we take perhaps too much for granted each day is in many ways a modern miracle. Indeed, whilst a good proportion of the world still suffers from insufficiency, we inhabitants of the richer parts of the planet tend instead to suffer from conditions related to excessive consumption: diabetes, obesity, heart disease, various cancers and so forth. This glut of food has been enabled by a number of factors, which principally stem from how we have modified the global ecosystem, how we have manipulated its resources to serve our own selfish ends, and how we treat each other. Some commentators have observed, based on the energy intensity of modern intensive food production systems, that contemporary agriculture is little more than the inefficient conversion of petrochemical energy into edible forms of energy.[3] And it is not just land area that is becoming a limiting factor to our capacity to feed a burgeoning population, including its booming, resource-hungry middle class, but also the availability and reliability of water and essential nutrient chemicals such as phosphorus.

---

[2] Diamond, J. (2005). *Collapse: How Societies Choose to Fail or Succeed*. Penguin Books: London.

[3] von Weizsäcker, E. Lovins, A.B. and Lovins, H.L. (1997). *Factor Four: Doubling Wealth, Halving Resource Use — The New Report to the Club of Rome*. Earthscan: London.

The sustainability challenges associated with future food security are immense. Some of the issues to be confronted are fiendishly technical, whilst others relate to reducing waste and better sharing of resources across the global community. Many more relate to equitable governance. But the first and most pressing need for food, drink, water, wood, cotton fibre and so many other global natural resources is simple awareness that they come from nature, return to nature and that we are, for all our sophisticated technological and trading enablers, dependent on nature for all of our needs. Awareness and respect for what nature does matters. So too does recognition that the ways we meet our needs and aspirations occur within nature's larger-scale processes and cycles, which should be a key point of reference for more informed, far-sighted and sustainable decision-making.

BALANCING THE ACCOUNT

We are all, I assume, familiar with how bank accounts work. Our accounts hold a capital amount allowing us to draw down money to do useful things including buying essentials such as food, paying service bills for water, telecommunications and the like, and treating ourselves to luxuries such as holidays and attendance of musical, sporting and other cultural events. But we also know that the rates and ways in which we use the money we draw down needs to be balanced with income-generating activities to ensure that the capital does not dwindle to the extent that it compromises the viability of the account and our ability to continue to benefit from it.

An essay published in 1798 by the Reverend Thomas Robert Malthus, *An Essay on the Principle of Population*, applied broadly similar logic to the problem of human population growth. The essay outlined the concept that potentially exponential growth in the human population would inevitably outstrip the linear growth rate of food supplies or other crucial resources. The concept was novel and powerful, leading to the coining of the adjective 'Malthusian' as a form of political and economic thought. Malthus saw two types of 'checks' operating to keep population growth in proportion to food supply: (1) 'preventive checks' including moral restraints reducing birth rates; and (2) 'positive checks' leading to premature deaths through factors such as disease, starvation and war, known as a 'Malthusian catastrophe' restoring population to a prior, sustainable level.

These ideas presented by Malthus have to be taken in the context of the time. The Industrial Revolution is generally considered to have taken root in Europe and later in the United States from around 1760, fomenting unprecedented mechanisation, manufacturing, wealth generation and, with them, rates of population growth. Humanity's capacities to exploit, transport and convert natural resources accelerated radically, along with major modification of rivers as also of landscapes through increasing mechanisation of farming. There was also a proportionate collateral generation of waste gases, matter and contaminated water, concentrated still further by accelerating urbanisation. In a brave new age of seemingly boundless creativity, production of novel and useful products, new markets and the imperial colonisation of lands from which resources could be plundered, Malthusian ideas presented an alternative, mathematically founded idea that there were biophysical limits.

Wider concepts of limits to growth imposed by the finite capacities of natural resources was brought starkly to bear on a still largely unaware world by publication in 1972 of *The Limits to Growth* report of the Club of Rome.[4] *The Limits to Growth* was based on a study using a World3 computer model to simulate the consequence of interactions between the earth and human systems, based on the five variables of: population; food production; industrialisation; pollution; and consumption of non-renewable natural resources. The authors noted that their predictions were purely indicative of the Earth-human system's behavioural tendencies, but presented three scenarios. Two principal scenarios saw 'overshoot and collapse' of the global system by the middle to the later part of the 21st century as humanity outstripped the re-newability of finite planetary resources, a third cluster of scenarios of a 'stabilized world' depending on stabilisation of the human population, the capital resource base and supporting economic factors. *The Limits to Growth* was published in the same year as the United Nations Conference on the Human Environment (also known as the Stockholm Conference), the first major conference on international environmental issues marking a turning point in the development of international environmental politics. Both had a powerful impact in a world of accelerating consumerism. This power was ably demonstrated by the energies expended in trying to debunk this view of biophysical limits by many major businesses and other opponents. In matters of timing, the illustrative modelled predictions were far from exact, for example, with the increasing market price of oil making exploration and exploitation of formerly uneconomic reserves feasible. Yet, oil reserves are ultimately finite and other factors — significantly including the finite capacities of the atmosphere and biosphere to safely dissipate and resorb excess carbon dioxide without environmental catastrophe — demonstrably illustrate the ultimately inescapable biophysical limits of Planet Earth's resources and processes.

It is in the essence of the concept of sustainable development that social and economic progress need to be integrated with environmental advancement as a fully integrated whole. As the ultimate wealth upon which future human security, prosperity and opportunity depends, we are demonstrably drawing down vastly more of nature's capital that it can bear whilst failing to reinvest in its renewability, with a very real risk that the Earth system will foreclose on our account. In a contemporary world in which 96% of all mammalian biomass on Earth is estimated as comprising humans and their livestock,[5] human consumption patterns are transgressing planetary boundaries beyond which abrupt global environmental change can no longer be excluded[6] threatening the viability of the natural world and the diversity of ways in which it is capable of supporting our continuing needs.

The dystopian trajectory of an unsustainable world, in which abuses of supporting ecosystems inevitably feed back into human prospects, are widely known and written

[4] Meadows, D.H., Meadows, D.L., Randers, J. and Behrens, W.W. (1972). *The Limits to Growth*. Universe Books: New York.

[5] Bar-On, Y.M. and Phillips, R. (2018). The biomass distribution on Earth. *PNAS*, 115(25), pp. 6506–6511. DOI: https://doi.org/10.1073/pnas.1711842115.

[6] Rockström, J. *et al.* (2009). Planetary boundaries: Exploring the safe operating space for humanity. *Ecology and Society*, 14(2), 32.

about. The key message here though is that paying close attention to our account with nature, much as we do our personal finances, can guide us towards means to modify the still substantially unchallenged ways in which we have wired society, spending or perhaps squandering what we draw down from our capital inheritance. We can use our now well-developed knowledge about ecosystem processes and their limits to test the implicit assumptions underpinning market and corporate governance systems founded at the time of the world's first Industrial Revolution, reflecting that they may no longer be appropriate for a sustainable pathway in the contemporary world. Our ecological knowledge can further inform us about wiser, more secure business and policy decisions that address our primary goals whilst also working in greater synergy with objective ecological realities that replenish our account. As with our own personal finances, we would be best advised to take care of the natural capital upon which our future collective wellbeing is founded.

Can we achieve this kind of profound transition in socio-ecological systems (a term defining the tightly interdependent nature of humanity with ecosystems)? Can we progressively move from today's implicitly degenerative cycle driven by liquidation of core supportive resources for largely short-term gain? Can we instead make a transition towards an explicitly regenerative cycle that not only balances exploitation with renewability but, if damaged ecosystems are allowed to regenerate, can actually expand their capacities to sustain safe and fulfilled lives? The answer to these questions is an unqualified 'Yes!' My 2020 book *Rebuilding the Earth: Regenerating Our Planet's Life Support Systems for a Sustainable Future*[7] collates examples from right across the world, from large landscape scale to microcosms in both dense urban and rural settings and from developed and developing nations, where solutions to problems have been founded not on technical fixes of localised symptoms but on protection, regeneration or emulation of ecosystem processes. These include reinstituting vegetative cover in the formerly fast-eroding landscapes of China's Loess Plateau and the Ethiopian Highlands, restoring soil fertility and water security bringing millions of people out of poverty. Other more technical, nature-emulating examples include 'green walls', sustainable drainage systems, urban trees and protected valleys bringing nature and its processes into dense cities to contribute to breaking down 'heat islands', addressing flood risk, removing pollutants from the air and providing culturally valuable 'green spaces'. Restoring connections between floodplains and river channels, and safeguarding important riparian, wetland and other habitats, forms a more natural basis for flood management and protection of the quality of raw water, yielding substantial, economically important benefits in terms of downstream flood risk and treatment of water abstracted for human uses, whilst simultaneously protecting vulnerable ecosystems of high nature conservation, fishery and amenity value. In these and many other exemplars, ecosystem processes form the foundations for solutions that give rise to many collateral co-benefits. Lessons drawn from these and many more diverse examples are distilled into principles that may be applied across all societal policy areas, ranging from addressing railway flooding to

---

[7] Everard, M. (2020). *Rebuilding the Earth: Regenerating Our Planet's Life Support Systems for a Sustainable Future*. Palgrave Macmillan: London.

peace-making and peace-keeping founded on security of shared resources, better protection of public health and the liveability of cities, and enhancement of soils and oceans securing global food security.

It is all a matter of understanding and balancing the account between us and nature. Importantly, it is also about balancing the account between us and those who will inherit this wonderful, supportive planet, historic and ongoing damage to which we can and must play an active role in reversing.

REMAINING ON A PLANET

The authoritative Millennium Ecosystem Assessment study by the United Nations,[8] the product of more than 1,300 scientists spread across 95 countries, explored the status of and trends in the Earth's major habitat types, the prognosis of this for continuing human wellbeing, and what we really need to start doing to avert future crises that may limit our capacity to live healthy and fulfilled lives. If you are interested, I commend these and related subsequent studies at national level, particularly the UK's National Ecosystem Assessment,[9] as worthwhile if slightly technical and rather scary reads.

But it is not just in science that our integral connectedness with nature is expressed. The essence of many animist or polytheistic belief systems (depending on your precise definition of these things), such as the Hindu, Shinto and Tao and many more tribal traditions, is recognition of the mystical and the spiritual in the everyday. In the Hindu doctrine, remarkable and often bemusing as it may be to those not steeped within it, the work of Brahma, the creator, is complete such that everything that exists, from the stars to the iridescence of a butterfly's wings right down to corpses and feces, embodies the spirit of the creator. In Shinto, *kami*, or spirit, is present in all that is natural or beautiful, whilst the essence of Tao (or Dao) is acceptance of a 'way' or a 'path' that harmonises one's will to 'become one with the tao' representing the flows of Nature. The sanctity of the natural world and our duty of care towards it also features in many other faiths. In all of these traditions, it is how people live their everyday lives that matters in honouring the spirit residing in all things, marking their faith, and in service to the great continuum of life and eventual fate.

However, one does not need to have any kind of religious faith nor a science degree to recognise, with systemic insight, that all things are connected in a kind of sacred dance. All things, throughout all of creation (whatever that means to you), including even the most mundane of everyday things, embodies meaning and value. The bottom line then is rediscovery of the unbreakable planetary roots of humanity and all of our business and other activities, the fascinating facts surrounding the ecology of everyday things, and that it is nature that supports our wellbeing throughout evolution, now and into the future. That awareness is enriching, inspiring, and may just be a spur and an illumination to help us live better, more respectful and sustainable lives.

---

[8] Millennium Ecosystem Assessment. (2005). *Ecosystems and Human Well-Being*. Island Press: Washington, DC.

[9] http://uknea.unep-wcmc.org, accessed 26 May 2020.

This sublimation — a transcendental awareness of the sublime residing within and arising from the mundane — evokes the presence of nature in the everyday. That is exactly what this book is all about as, when we recognise the value and importance of nature in the everyday, we will be embarked on the vital journey towards valuing the irreplaceable yet so commonly overlooked role of ecosystems in underpinning our future needs and aspirations.

Index